D1535506

Wildlife at Your Doorstep

Wildlife at Your Doorstep

text and drawings
by Glen Rounds

*An illustrated almanac of curious doings...
dealing with wasps...spiders...snakes...toads
...birds...ants...squirrels and other kinds of
small wildlife that can be found working at
complicated trades within sight of my doorstep.*

Holiday House · New York

1974

*This book was first published in 1958 by
Prentice-Hall, Inc. in a different format.*

77-529

Copyright © 1958 by Glen Rounds
Printed in the United States of America

LIBRARY OF CONGRESS CATALOGING IN PUBLICATION DATA

Rounds, Glen, 1906–
Wildlife at your doorstep.

SUMMARY: The author describes his observations
of the habits of insects, reptiles, birds, and other
wildlife within sight of his doorstep.
1. Zoology. 2. Animals, Habits and behavior of.
[1. Zoology. 2. Animals—Habits and behavior] I. Title.
QL49.R65   1974   591.5   73-17402
ISBN 0-8234-0238-X

Contents

Wildlife at Your Doorstep

The Cloak of Invisibility

In the Old Days, when almost every community had its share of magicians, witches, and sorcerers, there was always a brisk trade in charms and spells of one kind or another. One of the most popular was a magic cloak guaranteed to make its wearer invisible. They were handy things, to be sure, making it possible for timid folk to go about their affairs without interference from either friends or enemies.

Nowadays, however, the witches and sorcerers have mostly turned to fortunetelling, while the magicians idle away their time doing card tricks. But even so, the secret of invisibility is not entirely lost.

Fierce hunters prowl unseen around our doorsteps or fly in wide sweeping patrols through the weed patches and flower beds in the dooryards. Expert paper makers, potters, weavers, woodworkers, and masons work at their complicated trades in broad daylight beside the screen door or under the porch roof, with no one the wiser. Vicious but invisible battles are fought in plain sight on the clean-swept walk, and a flying squirrel sleeps undiscovered in the bird house nailed to the porch post. Nobody notices the dainty star-shaped tracks of the possum in the dust under the chinaberry tree or suspects that he spends his days in the honeysuckle tangle at the bottom of the garden.

Not every yard has a flying squirrel or a possum; but a surprising number do, even in the cities. And everywhere the wasps, beetles, spiders, and insects of a hundred kinds go about their complicated business almost unnoticed, unless they happen to fall into our bathtubs or our lemonade.

Of course, in the days when Magic was really Magic, it was common knowledge that for every charm there was a counter charm, if only you could find it. So, sooner or later the fellow wearing the Cloak of Invisibility was almost certain to come across someone with a stronger magic who could see him plain as day. But the wildlife populations in our dooryards have no special magic that makes them invisible—so we need no complicated counter magic in order to see them.

Nor is it necessary to strain our eyes and peer about like a man searching for the cat in a dark cellar. As a general thing people see only the things they happen to be looking for—everything else might as well be invisible. So the habit of seeing things we were not especially looking for is all the Magic we need. Once we have that, the Cloak of Invisibility these things wear loses much of its power, and suddenly we are able to watch them going about their affairs all around us.

A tiny sparkle in the bush beside the doorstep attracts our attention to an almost invisible thread of gossamer reflecting the early morning sunlight. And tracing this leads to the discovery of a small spider perched on the end of a twig.

At the moment he seems to be doing nothing at all— just sitting there trailing that fine kite string in the morning air. However, he is not frittering his time away. All wildlife —animals, birds, reptiles, or insects—live busy lives. But much of their business consists of watchful waiting, so anyone wanting to see them working at their trades must first of all learn the trick of patience.

This small spider is an early morning hunter on his way home to the knothole in the wall where he sleeps through the heat of the day. Of course he could simply climb down to the ground, walk the ten or twelve inches to the wall, then climb directly to his sleeping place.

But that is not his way. Instead, he waits quietly at the tip of the twig until small air currents begin to stir in front of the sun-warmed wall. Then he turns, raises his abdomen high, and spins out a thin, light strand of silk. It floats this way and that in unhurried fashion as he lets out more and more line. Time after time, just as the sticky tag at the end almost touches the wall, a change in the air current carries it away again. Sometimes the entire strand floats back and becomes entangled in the bush.

When that happens the spider patiently begins again. He spins a new line as often as necessary until at last the sticky end attaches itself to one of the boards across the way. After a couple of experimental twitches to make sure that it is firmly anchored, the spider pulls the line taut and makes his end fast to the twig at his feet. He now has a bridge high above the ground and he immediately starts cautiously across it. But halfway over something goes wrong. Either the anchor has come unstuck or the line itself breaks—it is difficult to tell which. At any rate, his bridge is down. But it is needless to look on the ground for the fallen spider. By nature he is something of a pessimist, and before setting out on such a trip he takes the precaution of attaching a strong lifeline to the twig at his feet, paying it out behind him, mountain-climber fashion, as he goes. So now he hangs safely at the end of his line, and when it stops swinging he climbs back, to float another bridge line across the gap. The second and the third ones fail also, but at last one holds and he makes his way safely across and disappears for the day.

The porch step is a grandstand seat overlooking an arena that is almost never empty. A slight movement of what seems to be an oddly shaped leaf demands attention, and a praying mantis suddenly comes out of his invisibility like a picture developing on a photographic negative. One wonders how he escaped discovery before.

The praying mantis is a killer who is seldom seen at his bloody work. He didn't get his name because of his nature but from his habit of holding his heavily armed front claws folded under his chin.

He is usually discovered only by accident, for he spends the greater part of his time motionless on some stem or twig, waiting for an unwary passerby to come within reach. His long legs and stick-like green body make perfect camouflage, and he is content to wait for days if necessary for his meals to come to him.

When the sun is too hot, or if it comes up to rain, he moves slowly, a fraction of an inch at a time, under the shelter of a leaf. Hanging motionless upside down or in other improbable poses, he is still in business. The mantis can turn his head to look backwards over his shoulder, so he is able to keep a careful watch all about as he waits. It makes little difference what comes by—a bumblebee, grasshopper, butterfly, or even another mantis, for he is not particular about whom he eats.

He usually plays a waiting game, but if he has to he will creep up on his victims as slowly and carefully as a stalking cat. When he is finally within sure killing distance, he shoots out his two big barbed claws for a firm grip. The victim may fight and struggle, but seldom escapes. The mantis draws him close and begins biting off dainty bits, chewing them carefully. His tiny, red-lipped mouth looks somewhat ridiculous in his green face, but it is armed with terribly efficient teeth. As he tears off bite after bite, chewing busily and spitting out small bits like a boy spitting watermelon seeds, his victim gradually struggles less and less.

When he has finished his meal the mantis drops the remains to the ground, and after casting a cold eye around at the bystanders, he washes himself as carefully as a cat. He is a neat, clean fellow, but he does give some people the creeps.

⋖§⋗

Except for such as the possum, the squirrel, and the birds, most of these creatures are very small game indeed.

But instead of ranging over miles of country as the lions, tigers, panthers, and such hunters do, these go about their business almost underfoot. Furthermore, the birds and insects have been around a long time and have learned intricate skills that make the larger animals' look simple. What animal could unravel the silk of a spider's egg sac or a cocoon to get silk to hang its nest as the vireo does? Who besides the wasp knows how to store meat, guaranteed not to spoil, for its young ones? What animal can make complicated traps and snares for catching game, or build bridges and rig lines to lift weights many times greater than its own as the spiders do?

And most of these will let you look over their shoulders as they work if you care to—a thing that tigers, lions, foxes, bobcats, and elephants do not allow, as a general thing.

Spring

The coming of spring to the dooryard is not a hit or miss affair by any means. All summer the place will operate as a highly organized food factory. And as with any factory, each shift of specialized workmen must appear—and each operation be started—at the proper time and in the proper order, or confusion results.

All winter the blue jays have roared and screamed about the place, making life miserable for the household cat and loudly discussing anybody whose activity happened to catch their attention. But with the coming of the first gentle late winter rains all this is changed. Except for occasional backsliding, they now speak only to one another, and in soft, mannerly voices. They go sedately about in pairs, or in fours and sixes, sitting by the hour in low branches carrying on their coaxing conversations.

Every now and again one flies off to perch on the very top candle of a pine tree and look admiringly about the area. Occasionally he will dig out some hidden grub or other treasure, let it fall, then tumble head downwards after it. At the last possible moment he opens his wings to break his fall, recovers his prize, and flies proudly off to offer it to one of his companions. This one may pass it politely to the next in line, who in turn may offer it to his less fortunate neighbor. A tidbit sometimes changes hands—or beaks— several times before it is finally eaten.

But this quiet time soon comes to an end. Even after all the work the local birds have done during the winter, there are still great quantities of berries left on many of the trees and bushes. And as every gardener knows, these left-overs must be cleared away to make way for the new crop.

So the robins are among the first of the spring workmen to appear. Gathered in huge flocks they work their way north, stripping the trees of leftover berries as they go.

The first few scouts move into town from the side nearest the swamp to look the situation over. Then, close behind them, comes a compact mass of hundreds more, working their way up the street, bush by bush and yard by yard. Gorged robins swarm round all the drinking places; and as the nearby water disappears, they travel farther and farther afield in search of more. Many stagger disgracefully from the effects of the half-fermented berries; but after a quick drink and a short rest, each one hurries back to join the main crowd at their work.

As the mockingbird listens to the sounds of the robin horde moving slowly up our block and into the yard next door, he begins to mutter querulously to himself from his perch on the chimney. He takes ownership of his territory most seriously.

Soon the first of the invaders drop into his yard to stand uncertainly around on the ground, waiting for reinforcements. Then a few more light on the telephone wire, and while the mocker is chasing these away others move onto the quince bush or perch on the arms and backs of the yard chairs.

For a while the mockingbird tries to be everywhere at once, but as the crowd increases he is forced to abandon first one bush and then another. Finally, hot and disheveled, he stands belligerently on the very tip of the holly tree, which is now a tiny island ringed round by hundreds of waiting robins. For a while the stalemate holds.

Then, as if at some secret signal, every robin in the dooryard springs into the air, and the holly tree disappears under a living blanket of rusty red and black. In seconds every branch and twig are loaded to the breaking point as the birds greedily harvest the winter-ripened berries.

No matter what the calendar says, the mocker knows spring is on the way.

During the winter several pairs of the various year-round birds have lived more or less peaceably in the dooryard. But now, with the newcomers moving in, there is bound to be some crowding. It is still too early for them to begin building nests, but there is much to do, nonetheless. Each pair must stake out and defend a territory large enough to furnish food for themselves and for their young ones.

So for a time there is a constant bickering over who shall stay and who must go.

✦§§✦

The one-eyed cardinal that builds in the bushes by the studio window every year claims the full width of the yard, including the thickets along the borders from the street to the grape arbor at the bottom of the slope. He pays no attention to the towhees, catbirds, thrushes, thrashers, and such birds when they look for nesting sites inside his territory. They all depend on different food supplies and so will not be in competition with him. But other cardinals are not welcome. Day after day he flies a looping, undulating patrol of his lines to make sure everybody understands who lives there. And if a claim jumper does appear, the old cardinal flies round and round after him in that same curious flight until at last the stranger goes away.

The tufted titmice occasionally interrupt their searching among the piles of dead leaves for cocoons and spider egg sacs to look about for possible nesting places also. Finding the bird house they've used for several seasons lying on the ground at the foot of the pine tree, they walk over it and peer inside while discussing the poor housekeeping of the flying squirrel that lived there during the winter. They complain at the tops of their shrill voices until it is hung up again where it belongs. Then, after several trips to inspect the inside, they go off to look elsewhere. Every year they do this same thing. They have a place in a hollow tree across the street where they raise their spring brood. About the first of July they'll come back to this box to lay the second lot of eggs. So why must they always make such a fuss here in March?

ஓஒ

By the time the leaves and first blossoms appear the birds have their summer territory pretty well laid out, but still they are in no hurry to start building, at least for a little while. The first insects have already begun to stir, but fantastic numbers will be needed to feed the nestlings when the season is really under way. So for a time the birds idle about, courting or resting while they wait for the new swarms of insects and caterpillars to begin their summer's work.

✺✺✺

Spring is a lonely time for the brown wasp queen. All winter she has hung by her jaws from a splinter in the cold dark between the walls of the house. And now, while the birds are courting and pairing off for the summer, she must build the foundations for a new wasp colony, and do it with no one to help her. A tiny *scrape, scrape* sound coming from where the spring sun is warm on the old floor boards of the porch is the first sign that she is up and about. Scraping fine shavings off the weathered wood, the wasp patiently chews them fine and mixes them with saliva to make paper pulp. When she has a small ball of material ready, she flies up and cements it to the underside of the porch roof, over the door. First she builds a stem half an inch long and then widens the bottom end. Working more delicately now, she outlines the bell-shaped foundations of half a dozen thin-walled cells that gradually take on honeycomb shape, although they are only a fraction of an inch deep. As each one is started, she lays an egg in it and then goes on about her patient paper making. She starts new cells around the walls of the first ones until she has a dozen, each with an egg cemented to the bottom. Apparently that is as many as she can take care of single-handed. But she continues her work of scraping pulp for paper and building the walls of the first cells higher and higher—or perhaps it should be lower and lower, since they hang open end downward.

After a few days the first of the old wasp's eggs hatches, and the caterpillar-exterminating machine slowly begins to move. The only food the old one touches is a little fruit juice or nectar from occasional blossoms, but this new grub is a meat eater. So the old wasp hustles off to search the mimosa leaves and the wisteria for the tiny caterpillars that are just beginning to appear. Bringing them home one at a time, she bites off pieces, then chews them to a pulp for the grub.

And as each new young one hatches, the old wasp's work increases so that she must spend long hours each day caterpillar-catching as well as papermaking. Then, when the first grub has grown to fill the finished cell, it spins a white cap to seal the open bottom in order to give itself privacy during the time it takes to change from grub to wasp. As each in its turn does this it means one less mouth for the wasp to feed, but she must still concern herself with paper work, completing the unfinished outer cells. Then one morning she has company. The first grub reopens the white silk door of its cell, and the first of the queen's daughters appears. She is a complete wasp, a worker, a trifle smaller than her mother. For a day or two she isn't much help around the house, since she spends much time cleaning and polishing herself. When she is hungry she sticks her head into a cell and taps the grub there with her antennae, urging it to spit up a drop of digested caterpillar broth.

But before long she begins to take over some of the housework. When the old one comes in with a caterpillar, the young one tears off bits, chews them up, and so helps feed the growing family.

Every day or two another new wasp appears, and before long they are not only helping with the caterpillar feeding but go hunting as well. Little by little they take over all of that work, and also start helping to make paper and to add new cells around the edges of the next. At first their paper is rough and streaky looking, but it seems to serve well enough, and they do better with practice.

As more and more workers hatch, the queen gradually turns over all the hunting and housework to them. She keeps herself busy laying eggs in the new cells they are continually building and in the old ones as they are vacated.

All through the hot days this caterpillar-exterminating machine, and the half dozen others around the house, grow in geometrical progression. And each day the demand for caterpillars increases.

While the birds and wasps are still going about their spring preparations in a half-hearted sort of way overhead, the small spider under the doorsill is at work in real earnest. In the three-inch space between the overhang of the sill and the bricks of the front step, she has built a frail and messy sort of web. Here and there are lines attached to the bricks below or to the wood above in a haphazard sort of way, and a seemingly patternless arrangement of braces and guys interlaces the upper parts of the upright lines.

The small spider is safe from the feet passing so close overhead, and the narrow space along the wall is a favorite game trail for insects going from one side of the yard to the other. So she does well enough, catching a few ants, small beetles, or an occasional fly. But nothing really gives her a tussle—until the day when she tangles with a box-elder bug.

He'd just been walking by, busy about some spring business of his own, paying no attention to the little web the spider had strung about the place. And even when one of his long hind legs brushed a sticky line and became entangled, he still seemed unconcerned. Without looking back, he braced his other feet and kicked about in a peevish way, like a man walking through a morning-glory vine. The web stretched and sagged, but as soon as one guy line broke in the tangle above, another took up the strain.

And then the little spider, attracted by the alarms her lines were sending, dropped down from her dark hiding place above. Swinging above the bug at the end of her lifeline, she looked the situation over, but what she thought about the size of the catch there is no telling. Perhaps she was only considering the odds or planning the best way to take care of such a big beef. To a disinterested observer it seemed that the best thing she could do was cut the creature free and be rid of him as soon as possible. Not only was her lack of experience against her, but it was obvious that neither she nor the fragile web had the strength necessary to deal with this monster.

However, the spider had other ideas. Going briskly to the top of her construction she dropped down again on another line, closer to the box-elder bug's trapped foot. Hanging there by some of her front legs, with her long hind ones she reached behind for a new silk throwing line. Flinging it much as a cowboy does a rope, she soon had the bug's entire foot swathed in a sticky-looking wrapping. One at a time she attached new lines to the trapped foot and anchored them firmly overhead.

Next, she hurried about through her overhead tangle of guys and braces, tightening some and adding new strands to others. As she worked, hauling in and taking up slack, the bug's leg was gradually drawn high up over his back. When this last chore was finished to her satisfaction, the spider disappeared again into her dark hiding place.

Perhaps she was tired and needed a nap, or maybe she was deliberately letting her victim tire himself out before she risked coming to close quarters. For now the big bug seemed to realize he was in trouble. Bracing himself and gripping the rough surface of the bricks with his five feet still free, he scrabbled and strained to pull away. From down at bug level, he looked like some armored monster from prehistoric times, caught in the tar pits. He neither sweated nor cried out, but his appearance gave the impression he was doing both.

After fifteen or twenty minutes of violent struggle, he managed to stretch the cords a quarter of an inch or a little more, and was perhaps encouraged. He may have thought that the spider had given him up, and that brawn and perseverance would free him from this mess. But just when it looked as if he might succeed, the spider came to work again. One by one she hauled on the lines until the bug was drawn so high he was able to get but the barest grip on the bricks with the feet that were still free. And then the spider left him to struggle some more.

At intervals of ten or fifteen minutes after that, she would come out of hiding and readjust the guy lines or add new ones as needed. And each time she lifted the tiring victim a little higher until at last he dangled free, unable to touch the ground with any foot.

Now it was time for the spider to get down to business. Swinging on one side or the other of the feebly struggling bug, she swung her sticky lassos. One by one she managed to entangle his remaining feet, draw them in close to his body, and lash them fast. After she had him securely trussed, she may have killed him with her poison fangs, but it was difficult to be sure. However, it made little difference, because alive or dead, he was now in no condition to give her any trouble.

Ordinarily, when the spider has finished trussing up a visitor, she quickly cuts away the entangling lines until he is hanging free. Then, taking a firm grip on his wrappings with her hind foot, she uses her others to climb hand over hand back to her dining room, for she dislikes to eat in public. But this was no small creature she could carry as a man carries a picnic basket, so she went about it in another way. Leaving the overhead lines attached, and adding a few new ones, the spider hauled in slack first on one set and then on another. One end of the tightly wrapped bundle would be raised a fraction of an inch as the sling lines were shortened, and then the other end would be brought level with it. Occasionally some of the rigging would give way, and she'd lose much of the distance she'd gained. But the spider would patiently replace the lines and go on with the slow business of hauling in slack and securing it.

It had taken her over an hour to subdue the bug and truss him up. And now she spent almost an hour more hauling him up a fraction of an inch at a time, until at last he was out of sight in the crack behind the sill.

You might think that much beef would last for weeks. But a couple of days later the box-elder bug's empty shell lay on the bricks beside the game trail where she had thrown it after sucking it dry, and the spider was in business again.

Birds

There is a widespread impression that all birds, without exception, instinctively know everything there is to know about nest building and go about it without hesitation or trouble. But like people, some birds have poor judgment, while others shilly-shally and have difficulty making decisions. Still others are bull-headed, know-it-all types that insist on doing things the wrong way no matter how much trouble it makes for them.

❧

The robin, the jay, the cardinal, and even the catbird, sometimes make a false start or two before going to work on a nest. But of all the birds in the yard, a pair of thrushes seemed to have the greatest difficulty picking a building site that pleased them. For days they looked at available places. One or another would sit for a while, swinging in a tangle of vine in the oak tree. Then they would look into the cherry tree, or walk along the level branches of the big pine in front of the house. Now and again one would squat as if sitting on an invisible nest and appear to be looking about to try the view.

At last they agreed on a place low in the magnolia and began carrying pieces of string, shredded bark, pieces of newspaper, cigar wrappers, and such trash, dangling it saddlebag-fashion over a branch for a foundation. But before they'd gotten far with that, they started two more constructions, both in the nearby pine tree.

Much of the first material the thrushes used in these foundations had fallen to the ground, so the yard was soon littered with odd scraps from the various nesting sites.

After a time, the thrushes gave up consideration of the magnolia, but they still couldn't decide between the two places in the pine.

By this time they were in a fever of indecision, pulling material out of one foundation and carrying it to the other. Eventually, they did make up their minds and began to work steadily on one location. Before long all the scraps on the ground had been picked up and re-used, as well as most of the material from the two discarded foundations. It appeared to be a terrible waste of work, but they seemed not to mind.

ଈୢୖଌ

Meanwhile, the red-eyed vireo had moved into the magnolia tree and was busy building her hanging, cup-like nest in a fork of one of the outer branches. Hunting out the egg sacs of spiders or cocoons of moths, she unraveled the silk threads and strung them by the hundreds over the supporting branches. Then she wove and knotted the hanging ends into a sort of purse below, a foundation that would support her nest of fine grasses and rootlets.

Later, on one of her trips to water, she passed through the thrushes' pine tree. Noticing that they were not home at the moment, she went over to inspect their unfinished work, much as people prowl through someone else's unfinished house. The foundation was complete, and on it the thrushes had built a ragged cup of long coarse grasses. Inside it was a lining of finer material of exactly the type the vireo needed for the second stage of her building. Later the thrushes would plaster this with a lining of mud and rotted leaves, but now it was still clean and neat.

So, taking a furtive look around to make sure the owners were still out of sight, the vireo pulled out bits of the inner material until she had all she could carry, then hurried back to weave it into her own nest.

One scarcely knows whom to trust, these days.

⊷§?§⊷

The birds always seem to be willing to try the new nest-building materials they find lying around the dooryard. The thrush gathers old bread wrappers, pieces of rags, and string to take the place of harder-to-get strips of bark, leaves, and such things for the foundation of her nest. The catbirds spend part of an afternoon tearing bits off a piece of old newspaper lying on the ground. And even the red-eyed vireo often uses bits of facial tissue instead of cocoons to decorate the outside of her nest.

These easy-to-come-by materials are great laborsavers and, used with restraint, are perfectly satisfactory. But one of the robins went too far with her modern ideas this spring. Finding a splendid supply of facial tissues where the garbage man had spilled a trash can, she used masses of them in the foundation of her nest. It was probably the quickest and easiest job she'd ever done, and when she was finished it was truly a nest to be proud of.

Her eggs were laid, and she'd been brooding for several days, when disaster struck in the form of an all-night rain. Within minutes the flimsy tissues began to disintegrate. And as the foundations shrank and slipped away the entire nest began to give and sag beneath the misguided bird, so that by morning it was a complete wreck.

Almost overnight there seem to be young birds everywhere. From every nest hungry, wide-open mouths blossom on the ends of stringy necks demanding food. Old ones go and come in stealthy fashion as they hustle to keep these new families fed. The thrashers drop to the ground and run like quick-moving shadows under the bushes so that it is difficult to discover the location of their nest. The cardinals come to their nest in the juniper tree by a roundabout series of stopping places, and the mocker runs the length of the scuppernong arbor, through the tangled top of the vine, before showing himself. The jays in the pine by the street come more directly but fly so softly and quietly that it is difficult to keep track of them.

The tufted titmice are more open about this business of raising a family. One sits now in the holly tree, skinning a hairy caterpillar to make it fit food for the young ones in the box. It is not a neat performance. The titmouse holds the creature to the branch with one foot, pulls off patches of hairy pelt with his beak, and flings them away like an inexperienced hunter skinning his first rabbit. Meanwhile, his mate sits on their lookout in a juniper snag close by, crying out loud encouragement or advice—or perhaps both.

The thrush comes silently up on the bricks of the kitchen terrace and catches a slug on its way to the damp mass of leaves under the spigot. She stuns and kills it on the bricks, then carries it out to the sand where she beats it some more, probably to get rid of its slime. When she considers it to be properly prepared, she parks the carcass on the rose trellis while she carries bite-sized pieces to the young ones.

Insects and caterpillars of all kinds are being slaughtered by the hundreds of thousands, for at this stage even the young of the seed- and fruit-eaters must have meat in order to get their growth.

But even with all this press of business, there is still time for the inquisitive ones to satisfy their curiosity about their neighbors. The catbird, on her way through the juniper from her nest in the chinaberry tree, hears the faint hissing of the cardinals' new-hatched young ones and decides to take a look. Pussy-footing through the tangle of fine branches, she peers over the edge of the nest for a minute, then softly flies off about her business before the cardinals come back. At the bottom of the lot, a starling sits on a twig just outside the doorway to the redbellied woodpecker's nest, peering in while the owner glares out at him. And everyone in the neighborhood, even the gray squirrel in her leaf nest in the old oak, sooner or later looks up to find herself eye to eye with one of the nosey wrens.

✌§§✍

People will tell you that birds take no nonsense from their young ones when it comes time to leave the nest and go out into the world. As soon as the young birds are able to put their feathers on straight, the old ones supposedly give them the old "heave ho," and from then on they are on their own to sink or swim.

But, as a matter of fact, the young ones usually leave home only because the nest will no longer hold them. And it is often a time of great worry and trouble for the old birds.

For some days before they leave the nest, the rapidly growing young birds find their quarters becoming more and more crowded. Each time one youngster changes his position the others are forced to rearrange themselves also.

A scattering of dark, ugly pinfeathers are beginning to give the bare bodies of the young birds a ragged look. And as the transparent feather casings on the small birds dry, they seem to itch, so they spent hours working at them with their beaks, freeing the feathers inside. Each day the young birds need more room for this job, but each day there is less, and the nest is in a constant gentle turmoil. And as both feathers and muscles develop, there is a growing need to stretch the legs and flap the wings or to stand on the edge of the nest for a look at the neighborhood while practicing balance. The youngsters really grow themselves out of house and home.

The day the young jays left their nest in the pine tree they started their preparations early in the morning. Standing for a few minutes at a time on the outside edge of the nest, teetering and flapping, they would look boldly about for a moment or two. Then, seeming almost overcome by the size of this outside world, they would hurriedly scramble back to the very bottom of the nest and not stir for half an hour or more. Perhaps they were exhausted by the exercise and needed rest.

At this time, the old birds came with food occasionally but not on the same schedule as on the days before. Much of the time they left the young ones alone but kept a watchful eye on them from across the street. When there was any sound from the nest, they answered in soft, encouraging voices. And all during the day the young ones divided their time between these small exercises and periods of sound sleep.

About noon the boldest one, after much indecisive teetering on the edge of the nest, at last made a prodigious leap to a twig at least three inches away. With a great flapping of his half-feathered wings, he managed to balance himself safely and look about the world from this new vantage point. Then, edging along the twig a little way, he made another fluttering jump back to the main branch.

From there he hustled back into the nest for another rest. Several times he made the same trip, once even going on to a third branch a foot away to meet one of the old ones coming in with rations. But none of the others would take such risk.

It was almost sundown before the leaving actually got under way. Dropping onto the outer end of the branch with food, the old ones would watch the nest for a bit, then fly away without having gone any nearer. After this had happened once or twice, the bold young one learned to hurry down the branch to be fed; and later the others followed him. So before long all these young birds were traveling freely on that high, airy walkway.

Later, the old jays moved into some nearby pines across a six-foot gap from the branch where the young birds sat. While the parent birds spoke coaxingly, the young ones, looking neat and fresh in their white under-feathers and blue tops, teetered on the branch.

After a time the leader stretched himself high and then fluttered into violent, clumsy flight. Handicapped by a lack of tail feathers, his flying was more serviceable than graceful, but he landed safely in the neighboring tree. And, one after the other, two youngsters finally followed him while the old birds continued to speak encouragement.

This left one small jay alone on the branch—but he simply could not make up his mind to take that risky flight. Several times he teetered and fluttered on the very edge of going, then, at the last minute, refused.

Meanwhile, the others were being led from branch to branch and tree to tree, deeper into the safety of the vacant lot next door.

One of the old ones, after trying unsuccessfully to coax the timid child, finally went off, then came back a little later to feed him. But as soon as he'd eaten, the young bird hustled back to huddle in the very bottom of the nest again.

The old one seemed much disturbed by this, but after all, there were the others to look out for and get settled on safe perches for the night. Once or twice she came back to see if this backward offspring had changed his mind. Each time he would go to the jumping-off place, look about, and then hurry back to the safety of the nest; so his mother went away at last and left him alone for the night.

In the morning he was still in the nest. Now and again one or both old ones came back for a few minutes and fed him or tried to reason with him. It wasn't until late in the morning that he finally left the branch. And then it was only to flutter weakly down to the ground. There the old ones fed him again. Then, coaxing and chivying him by turns, they guided him as he hopped clumsily across the street and into the shelter of some bushes. But he seemed weak and puny, so the chances are he soon died or was caught by some cat or snake.

This is indeed a sad sort of story, but it is not an uncommon one, for in a surprising number of these bird families there is a problem child.

ᴥᎦᎧᴥ

The cardinals' nest was in a high bush beside the terrace, and when their young ones were ready to leave it, they had a wide stretch of grass to cross to reach a bush by the mimosa tree. From one branch to another the young cardinals worked their way, higher and higher into the mimosa. Then, after a rest, it was a simple matter to fly across the four- or five-foot gap to the chinaberry behind the studio. One by one, they successfully made the trip, finally perching proudly in the cool and airy shade just outside of the second-story windows.

And then it was the turn of the last little cardinal. He hopped up into the first branches of the bush as the others had done—but there he froze. Holding the slender twig in a death grip, he refused to go higher in spite of all coaxing and encouragement. After ten or fifteen minutes he relaxed a little and dropped back to the ground, where he was fussed over and fed.

But each attempt to get him moving up the tree ladder to the spot where the other three waited ended in failure. As soon as he found himself more than a foot off the ground, he reacted much as people do who are afraid of high places.

And, as sometimes happens, even among people, the

neighbors made things even more difficult. The wrens are nosey fellows always, and when they came on the young cardinal hanging to an upright stem of the privet hedge and refusing to go either up or down, they came right up to discuss the business. Seeming to pant and strain to maintain his grip on the slippery bark, his small ragged crest sticking out in all directions, the young cardinal made no move as these loud neighbors hopped about in the bush, examining him from all sides.

After a time the wrens left off their inspection to attend to their own affairs. And at dusk the old cardinal led him across the lower end of the yard and finally left him for the night in a honeysuckle tangle. Perhaps he felt better about the bird business the next day, but there is no way of knowing.

Sometimes the business of getting the young ones from the nest to safety elsewhere turns out to be difficult even when each is strong and willing.

The first young jay to leave the nest in the juniper made straight for the thicket of big bamboo at the edge of the lot. It was only a ten- or twelve-foot flight, but when the young bird, flapping and wobbling mightily, tried to find a perch, he was in trouble. The slender bamboo branches were too small and limber to support a bird his size. And when he tried to grip the upright trunk, his claws slipped on the smooth, hard surface, so he slowly slid to the ground.

While he struggled with his trouble, the others followed him, and in a little while there were four confused small birds on the ground under the bamboo.

Even after the young birds had become discouraged, and probably tired as well, they only went to a pile of broken branches half way between the thicket and the chinaberry. Arranging themselves on the highest part of the pile of dead wood, they sat and faced the unfriendly bamboo, ignoring the easily climbed tree just behind them.

It took the old birds three or four hours and endless worry to get them turned around and up into the safety of the chinaberry.

Even with birds there seems to be difficulty convincing the young ones that their elders know best.

Mud Dauber

In the summer the dark corners of the hot, airless sheds and lofts vibrate with insistent buzzing during the middle parts of the day as if dozens of tiny high-speed saws were working their way through knotty timber. The mud dauber, singing (or complaining) as she works at her plastering, is the one responsible for the mysterious sounds.

The mud dauber is a neat, slender, black wasp with a few small spots of bright yellow on her thorax for trim. Her legs are dressed in alternating sections of yellow and black, making for a very gay appearance when examined closely, and her abdomen is carried on a slender stalk well out of the way of her work.

People see her going about her affairs and think what a fine life she leads with nothing to do but drift from flower to flower, loafing in the sun. But as a matter of fact, she is a very hard worker and a skillful one. Before the summer is out she must build a separate apartment for each of her many children and lay in provisions enough to last each one until he or she is ready to go out into the world and be self-supporting.

Flying here and there, inspecting places under the eaves, crawling through knotholes and cracks to get behind the walls, the mud dauber scouts for a location for her building. Air conditioning is not for her. The stifling heat of an attic suits her fine, and while she will occasionally build out in the light, she prefers a dark corner.

Once she has settled on a building site, she flies off for material and soon comes back with her first ball of soft mud. She holds it between her jaws with some of its weight supported by her two front legs. Sticking the mud to the wall, she starts her buzzing and her work at one and the same time. She pulls and trowels the mixture with her jaws, first plastering a foundation for the inch-long horizontal tube she will build. When that is done, she begins with a smaller than dime-size cup, raising the edges in successive narrow bands.

The inside of the tube is slightly larger than her body, so after each course of masonry is laid, she goes inside and smooths the surface of the interior. Coming back outside, she inspects her work, taking off a bit here and putting it there.

She works with messy material but has no intention of looking bedraggled herself; so each time, before flying off for another load, she spends considerable time cleaning up. She polishes her antennae, washes her face and all around her head. Her legs she cleans next, rubbing them against one another until every bit of mud is gone. Then she lifts her abdomen high and polishes and scrapes it—top, bottom, and sides—with her long legs. When she is convinced there is not a speck of dirt on her anywhere and that she shines all over, she takes off again.

When the apartment is finished, she still cannot knock off for a vacation. For now she must turn hunter and search the weed patches and bushes for spiders to store in the cell with her egg.

Among naturalists there seems to be considerable disagreement about whether mud daubers lay their eggs on the first spider in the cell or on the last. One book says one thing and one another. But the mud dauber here always attaches the egg to the first spider she brings in.

In and out, around and about, you can see her working in the hot sun. The competition is stiff, for it seems that everybody is hunting spiders. Searching the undersides of leaves, clumps of grass, and along the walls of buildings, she catches her share.

As soon as it hatches, her young one will need fresh meat, so she uses the mud cell as a live tank in which to keep the spiders until butchering time. But ordinary live spiders would be more than the small wasp larva could handle. So after she has caught her victim, the dauber takes him in hand and stings him just a little. She seems to operate much as the dentist does with his novocain needle. The spider stays alive but dopey; even after some days he will move only a little when touched. Each one she catches must be carried home and stuffed into the mud tube. There is no specified number of spiders she needs—she keeps bringing them until the tube is full. Spiders, however, vary in size, so she may need anywhere from six to twenty for each cell. Small spiders are the most welcome, but she is not one to turn down a large one if she can possibly carry it. So sometimes her trip home is made in short, straining stages with frequent periods of rest between.

When the last spider has been caught and has been butted gently into place with her head, the mud dauber brings still more mud with which to seal the entrance to keep light—and robbers—away.

Occasionally she may take as long as a couple or three days to build a cell, if weather is bad or other things interrupt, but under ordinary conditions she will build one in two or three hours. And her spider hunting is subject to much the same time variation. But however long it takes, the mud dauber usually leaves her door open until the last spider is stored away. As a general thing, once she seals up a door she never reopens it.

But during a spell of dry, windy weather, which apparently made spiders difficult to come by, the wasp building on the underside of my drawing board changed her ways. The cell on which she had been working was finished about eleven in the morning, and she brought her first spider in an hour later. But by five o'clock, she'd added only two more, small ones at that, so that the place was less than half filled. Before I quit work, she sealed the entrance and went away to wherever it is she spends her leisure time. The next day was cool, rainy and damp, so none of the wasps around the place worked. The following day was hot after the rain, and about ten o'clock in the morning the wasp returned and unsealed her partially filled cell. In an hour she brought in three good-sized spiders, thus filling the place completely. After sealing the cell again, she wasted no more time but immediately started work on a new cell.

After the wasp has built three or four cells side by side, she begins a second story. By the time she finishes, she may have anywhere from five to a dozen cells, all neatly joined to one another. Sometimes they will all be of the same color, the mud from which they are made having come from one particular place. Other times, if conditions have changed, the wasp will have used mud of several different colors. One especially handsome job I can see as I look up from my work contains two cells of a nondescript gray, one of almost pure whiteness, another a pale gray-blue, one of ochre, and still another almost a tile-red.

It is a tremendous amount of work the mud dauber does in the course of a summer. And all of it for children she'll never recognize as her own if she meets them later on in the weed patches. Of all those hundreds of spiders she catches, not one makes a meal for her.

While she goes on about her other affairs, her young one will hatch in the dark nursery and begin to feed on the fresh meat stored alongside him. One by one, he'll work his way through the dormant spiders, growing into a fat, gray, grub-like larva as he does so. When the spiders are gone, he spins himself a thin brown cocoon, then settles down to wait for the change from grub to wasp.

৩৪়৵

Later in the summer, another wasp appears in the mud dauber's territory over my drawing board. She is a somber lady, dark blue or black, with no touch of bright color. She too brings up her young ones in clay cells stuffed with spiders.

By now a good many of the mud dauber's young ones have hatched and gone away, leaving the building they occupied in good repair, except for the small escape hatches they drilled on their way out. The blue wasp looks these vacant places over, gnawing at the dried mud to enlarge the doorways.

She is by no means the industrious character the mud dauber is, and she seems slow to make up her mind. One opening after another is inspected, this activity being interspersed with long spells of just sitting. When the blue wasp does make up her mind and settles on an apartment, she is faced with a housecleaning job first off. It is probably not a pleasant job, but it is easier than building a house for herself. Perhaps the messiness of the undertaking is why she shows so little enthusiasm for the business. But sooner or later she sets to work. Going inside, she gathers up a load of trash—scraps of the thin brown sleeping bags the larvae have left behind, legs of used-up spiders, and such assorted material. When she has gathered what she can carry, she backs slowly out and flies off for a few feet before letting her load drop. Once this part of her work is done, she goes about hunting spiders to fill the place, as the mud daubers do. But even here she fails to show much enthusiasm. She may bring in a spider or two, then take some mud to seal the entrance temporarily until another day.

By ten o'clock on a summer morning the upstairs of the studio is usually hot enough to please the most exacting wasp, and the mud daubers come and go in a steady traffic pattern. Carrying mud for building, or spiders for stocking nurseries, they seem intent on making the most of every favorable minute.

But the blue mud wasp takes a different view of matters. Undisturbed by the heavy traffic, she loafs around until nearly noon on one of the borrowed buildings she is remodeling. Then, going outdoors for a drink of water, she comes back and soaks a spot on the doorway of the cell she closed yesterday. As the mud softens, she begins to dig it away until she has reopened the doorway to a size she considers suitable, then goes off to hunt.

Presently she flies back with a spider, but on her first attempt to land she loses her footing and drops to the floor. It is plain that something is troubling her but a close look gets an unfriendly stare in return, along with the discovery that she has a gob of spider web tangled around one of her hind feet.

I watched as, after each failure, she hung on with three feet—her two front ones were helping support the spider gripped in her jaws—while she tried to scrape off the tangle encasing her other foot. Each attempt resulted in failure, but she seemed unwilling to lay her victim down and do the job right. Instead, she would change her grip, turning and rolling the spider to get his legs into a neat package that would go through the doorway. At last she managed to get him started, tail end first. After that it was a simple matter to squeeze him through her narrow door, then to push him firmly into place on top of the other spiders already in the cell.

ఌఀౙఄ

Except for my watchfulness, the blue wasp's last nursery enterprise would have ended in a double tragedy. In her usual dilatory way, she had cleaned out another abandoned mud dauber's apartment, carried in one small spider, and laid her egg before sealing the doorway. The next day she loafed, not liking the weather, and didn't carry on her business until the day following. Hunting seemed to be bad that day—only a single spider and it a small one. One day later, after her usual noontime rising, she reopened the nursery door, then went out to capture her third spider. Her luck was good; she was back with a small one within ten minutes. Then she immediately hurried off to bring in another.

What misfortune overtook her there is no way of telling. Maybe she was careless and got entangled in some spider's web; maybe a flycatcher caught her, or one of the beetles that lie in wait in dark places. But whatever happened, she never came back.

All that afternoon and all the next day her doorway remained open. After the second full day it was plain she was never coming back, and a look inside the still unsealed mud cell showed the new larva looking expectantly for something to eat. Except for a scatter of inedible spider legs, his cupboard was entirely bare. Obviously, something had to be done. Also, it was plain that this would be no simple matter of feeding the larva warm milk from a bottle or medicine dropper as one does with orphaned rabbits, squirrels, and such creatures. This fellow needed spiders, but even if I were to catch one, I was not equipped to prepare it properly. For while the young wasps demand live meat, they are not strong enough to deal with a spider who is naturally unwilling to cooperate. The old wasp stings him just enough to tranquilize but not to kill him. So, at first, it seemed I had a problem of a certain difficulty —and books on how to raise young wasp grubs by hand are not easy to come by.

However, the place was full of mud daubers bringing properly paralyzed spiders to storage. Of course, putting the orphaned larva to nurse with another young one, as is often done with calves, lambs, or pups, was obviously impractical. So undoubtedly the next best thing was to search out a mud dauber whose cell was not yet entirely filled and to borrow from her. Working carefully with tweezers while the lady was away, it was a simple matter to take a fat spider out of the cell and present it to the orphan.

This seemed to be perfectly satisfactory to the larva, so at intervals during the afternoon the mud dauber's store was robbed and the loot presented to the motherless one until there appeared to be enough food to last him through his spider-eating time.

What the mud dauber thought there is no knowing, but as her spiders disappeared one by one, she continued to make trip after trip, bringing fresh spiders to replace them.

She probably heaved a sigh of relief when, at long last, she finally did get a proper supply put away without interference and was able to seal up the door.

Anyone looking at an abandoned mud dauber's nest can see the neat, round escape hatches in the end of every cell. But who makes this doorway? Does the young wasp do it, or does the old one return and release her children at the proper time? Prying a finished set of mud cells off the wall and putting them in a jar on my work table seemed a simple way to find the answer. But even after this was done, the creatures had a way of doing this business when I was busy elsewhere.

A persistent gnawing sound gives the first warning that something is about to take place. Often, too, before the wasp starts work on the door to the outside world she has never seen, a muffled buzzing comes from inside the cell. Perhaps this sound comes from some action that helps her to free herself from the shreds of the cocoon, or maybe it is a way she has of strengthening her new wings while still in the privacy of her dark chamber. At any rate, it is a surprising thing to have a tightly sealed mud cell suddenly begin to buzz and vibrate as you hold it in your hand.

The gnawing sound goes on for a considerable time before there is any sign on the outside. And then a dot of dark shows in the dried mud at the end of the cell and quickly enlarges to half the size of a pinhead. A very close examination will reveal a sharp, black, sickle-shaped mandible reaching out.

And then the unhurried gnawing starts again. A fine black line begins to grow out from the dot, the first of the narrow cuts the new wasp will make, radiating from the first tiny hole. When the wasp has cut a slot along two sides of a small triangle, the mandible appears again at the hole; it begins to pry out pieces of the weakened tip of the cell. From then on, by means of alternate prying and cutting, the work advances rapidly, and in a few minutes the wasp has a neat round hole the size of her slim body.

First, her head comes out for a quick look around, and then a brand-new wasp walks into the light. She is complete and ready to go, and as soon as she has cleansed a few bits of dust from her antennae, she flies to a perch on the table, there to clean and polish her whole body before going away to start the business of being a mud dauber wasp.

Diggers

The sunny patches of ground in front of the doorstep grandstand are favorite places for many of the wasps who dig in the ground. These are solitary ones, like the mud daubers, and they also store live meat with their eggs to feed young ones they'll probably never see. They are of many sizes and colors and specialize in many different kinds of game.

ᭂᔆᔆᭂ

A slim black wasp, long-legged and carrying her abdomen high and dainty on a long thin stem, came to inspect the dooryard this morning. After looking at various possible locations she finally chose a few square inches of bare dirt in the litter under a bush and started digging.

Naturally, when you dig a hole there is dirt to be disposed of, but she has no mind to have it piled in her dooryard for the neighbors to see. Buzzing and muttering to herself, she loosens a mouthful, then picks it up, backs out of the shaft and flies off to dispose of it some distance from her workings. Flying at an altitude of six inches or so, she flings the loads away with considerable force, so that they make a distinct rattling sound when they strike the dry leaves. Some dirt she drops in one place, some in another, so that nowhere is there any sign of digging.

But even so, three or four of the tiny gray and black flies that hang around all wasp diggings soon discovered her activity and watched from a safe distance.

Working without pause, except for short spells when she cleaned and polished herself, she had the hole finished in about an hour. Then she plugged the entrance with a chip of bark and some loose dirt carried from near by, but she made no attempt to conceal it and flew off.

Two or three hours later she came around the corner, dragging a caterpillar twice as long as herself. Gripping it by the neck with her jaws and holding her head high, she straddled the creature so it trailed between her legs on out behind her. Dropping it six inches or so from home base, she hurried ahead to open the door and make last-minute changes in the interior, probably to make sure the bottom chamber was big enough for her victim. Then she hurried out and, gripping her friend by the nape of the neck, she walked backwards to her door and went down inside, dragging her load behind her. It took only a few moments to arrange the caterpillar in a neat coil in the chamber, fasten an egg to him, and come again to the surface.

Gathering bits of dirt here and there, she would throw a few shovelsful down the shaft, then descend to tamp them firm with her head before going after more. When the hole was filled to the top, packed and smoothed, she started the business of hiding her place. Running in this direction and that, she searched for tiny sticks, big grains of sand, or shreds of leaves to scatter over her diggings.

Some distance off she found a small acorn and picked it up. Using her mandibles like a pair of tongs to carry it home, she jammed it firmly in place exactly on top of the spot where the shaft opening had been. Then she searched for small, fiber-like roots that lay exposed on the ground.

Pulling and tugging to find pieces that would come loose, she dragged them back to add to the litter.

When she was finally satisfied that there was no sign anywhere of her digging, she circled the place a few times for a last look and then went away. The gray flies had come back just as she started filling up her doorway and had watched her again from their safe distance. As soon as she left they hurried to the spot and ran this way and that to see if perhaps there was a gap in her work. They had hoped so much to get a chance to lay their own eggs on her caterpillar; but she had outwitted them, so they soon swallowed their disappointment and flew off to look for some other business.

Like a person trying to arrange the furniture in the living room, wild things are often plagued by an inability to make decisions.

A spider hunter, the tiny black wasp with the red band around her abdomen, spent an hour or more searching the ground between the scattered weeds in front of the porch. She investigated small clods, looked between the stems of the crab grass, and peered under each fallen leaf and tiny bundle of pine straw. Back and forth she hurried, zigzagging this way and that over an area probably six feet square. Now and then she stopped to polish her antennae and clean her feet and legs, but otherwise she showed no hesitation. It was plain that she knew exactly what she was about.

Just when it looked as though she was wasting her time, she suddenly darted under a small stick and came out with a spider a little larger than the head of a kitchen match. Apparently she didn't sting him on the spot, but hustled him under a pile of pine straw to do her dirty work safe from prying eyes.

When she'd finished whatever it was she had to do to quiet him, she left her victim hidden and came out to look for a place to dig the burrow which would be her nursery. But now she seemed nervous and undecided. After a number of false starts, she finally decided on a location a couple of feet from where the spider was hidden.

Before starting work she hurried back to get him. Almost all of the other digging wasps drag their victims, but she picked hers up firmly by the middle and carried him well off the ground. Back at her diggings she placed him carefully on some tiny clover leaves half an inch off the ground, out of the way of the ants, and began to dig. The shaft was nearly an inch deep when, on one of her frequent trips to inspect the spider and to make sure there were no ants about, she somehow dislodged him and he fell all the way to the ground. This seemed to distress her, and she jittered around, inspecting him carefully for damage, then ran back and forth between the drugged spider and the burrow. Apparently deciding at last that action was needed, she took a firm grip on him and after running a few steps one way and then another, she hauled him up a stem of crab grass and laid him on one of the flat leaves.

To me this seemed an ideal place. There was no danger of his falling off, and he was a good inch higher off the ground than he'd been before. But the wasp must have thought otherwise. She ran about some more, climbing various grass stems in the neighborhood. Then she hurried back for her spider, hauling him down to the ground, then up another grass stem and onto a curling leaf three or four inches higher than the one he'd just occupied. But this leaf was much more limber than that of the flat crab grass, and as soon as she laid the spider down, he began to slip. Each time she managed to recover him before he fell, but before long it became plain to her that this dodge wasn't going to work. Back on the ground again, she seemed to do some more worrying; then she carried her spider to the unfinished burrow and tried to stuff him into it. But the passage was much too narrow, and when the wasp discovered this, she went to pieces entirely. She ran off, making short dashes of only a foot or so in various directions, hurrying back after each trip for another attempt at stuffing the spider into the burrow. If a wasp ever wrings its hands, she was wringing hers.

At last she again picked the poor fellow up and carried him under an oak leaf lying on the ground two feet away. Coming out once more into the open, she ran about over the top of the leaf, examining it carefully. Then she went underneath, brought out her spider, and laid him on the very middle of the leaf. For the next ten minutes or thereabouts all was confusion. She'd travel about inspecting grass stems and tiny sand plots for a bit, then suddenly hurry away to carry the spider to a new place—to wait for her while she continued this curious search. She had carried him around the three sides of a six-foot triangle and wasted half an hour before she finally settled on a place and started a new digging.

Up to now she had been very careful of the spider, carrying him well off the ground and dusting him off occasionally. But when she began her new excavation, she dropped him right beside her work so that he was soon half covered with the dirt she was kicking out behind her. But paying no attention to this, she worked away, cutting the earth loose with her jaws, lying on her side or even on her back to shape the walls and tunnel. She wasted no time, and when she had a shaft about two inches deep with a small chamber at the end, she backed out, yanked the spider out from under the dirt that almost hid him, and without any attempt to dust him off, hauled him out of sight. It took only a minute or so to arrange him in the round chamber underground, lay her egg, and cement it to the spider's body. Then she carefully filled the hole, tamped the dirt firmly in place, and flew away without the usual circlings and second looks at the place.

She had really spent a dreadfully wearing morning on this job.

Still another wasp occasionally stages entertainments close to the grandstand seats on the back steps—a tiny, solid black one this time, a spider hunter also.

When she has made a tunnel a couple inches deep and a little smaller than a lead pencil, she hollows out a chamber at the bottom of the tunnel to fit the spider. Dragging him inside, she stows him away and then lays her egg, attaching it firmly to a tender spot so that when the larva hatches he will not have to go out or even search around the room for something to eat. This one fat spider will furnish food enough to last all through his childhood.

With her head and shoulders above ground, she reaches out her front feet and rakes some dirt into the hole she is standing in. And then comes a curious performance: instead of turning to pack the fill with her head and jaws as the other wasps have done, she suddenly begins to vibrate up and down for all the world like a man operating a pneumatic drill. It isn't until she nears the end of the job and is working entirely out in the open that it is possible to see what she is doing. Bracing herself, her legs spread wide, she hammers the loose dirt with the tip of her abdomen, moving so fast her whole body blurs.

The earth she has taken out of the hole is a slightly different color from that on the surface of the ground, so for the final bit of filling she searches around, gathering a bit of surface dirt here and a little more there and tamping it carefully until all trace of her digging is gone.

When she is satisfied with this she goes to work on the left-over pile of dirt. Scratching it under her body, kicking it out behind her, and carrying obstinate bits in her jaws, she scatters it far and wide, leaving no traces to attract the attention of any nosey parker.

৯৯৯

Another small hunting wasp with orange body and dark-blue wings occasionally searches the porch floor and the undersides of the porch chairs. Running with her head down like a hound on a trail, she zigzags this way and that, unnoticed by the owners of the feet she inspects in passing. Finding nothing on the porch, she flies a few feet to drop down on the clean-swept walk to continue her hunt. On short side trips into the grass she looks under fallen leaves and small bundles of pine straw, besides investigating any holes or cracks in the ground. As she works she continually twitches her wings, and occasionally, for no apparent reason, she jumps an inch or so straight up in the air.

Most of her hunting is done on foot, but she flies with great suddenness from one location to another and covers a surprising amount of territory. No matter how carefully one marks her flight, sooner or later she simply dips a wing and disappears as suddenly and completely as a flying saucer.

But by keeping a close lookout it is occasionally possible to see her coming home with her victim, for she likes to do her burying in the dry, loose dirt under the house. Getting such a huge creature home is no small chore, even now that he's completely paralyzed and harmless. But the wasp doesn't give the matter a second thought. She turns him on his back to keep the eight legs from catching on things, takes a firm grip on one of his feelers, and drags him inch by inch across the yard.

Naturally she cannot look over her shoulder without letting go of the spider, so her progress is often a series of small mishaps. First thing she knows she's backed herself into the dark shadows under a magnolia leaf and has to turn around and get her burden back out. Or she backs into a small tangle of grass that lets her through without trouble but holds the spider back. Every few feet she drops her load and hurries to the foundation of the house, up the brick wall, and disappears through a crack in the mortar—probably checking to make sure that all arrangements are in order so there'll be no delay when she finally gets her spider home. Hurrying back to where she left her victim, she looks him over carefully to see that no harm has come to him in her absence.

Like all of us who carry food about outdoors she has her troubles with ants, and if she finds one messing around her spider, she goes after him with her jaws and either flings him clear or throws him back under her body where she appears to try to sting him. The ant seldom seems to be much damaged by this business, but as soon as she lets him loose he leaves the neighborhood without delay. And after a quick look all around to see that none of his friends is about, the wasp goes back to her tugging and hauling. Coming at last to the foundation wall, she does not hesitate but climbs head downward with the spider swinging below her. Sometimes getting her feet tangled in old cobwebs, she loses her footing and falls. Or the spider may slip from her grasp, so that she must go down and start the whole business over. But sooner or later, no matter how many setbacks she may have, she succeeds in hauling him out of sight between the old bricks.

Inside the dark space under the house she carries her spider to the ground at the bottom of the wall and carefully lays him down while she hurries off for another look at the place she has selected for his burial. After making sure the place is suitable, she brings the spider and puts him down where she can keep an eye on him while she works. The dirt here is very dry and loose, and well mixed with small pieces of coal, bits of gravel, and other trash. A tunnel would cave in as fast as she dug the dirt out, so the wasp simply digs a pit to bury the spider in. By the time she has finished, it is a little more than three quarters of an inch deep, but due to the constant caving it is nearly two inches across the top. Now that the depth suits her she spends a little time packing and shaping the bottom. Then she brings her spider and puts him in the bottom. But apparently she isn't satisfied with the fit, for she drags him halfway up the bank and makes some more changes in the shape of the burial place. When that finally suits her, she starts wrestling with the spider until finally he is on his back at the bottom of the pit with two-thirds of her body underneath. At first this looks like an accident, but later it develops that the wasp is busy laying an egg under there and cementing it tightly to the spider's hide. When she is finished she comes out from under and immediately begins pulling dirt down from the sloping sides of the pit and packing it under the edges of the carcass. At intervals she stops to pack this fill, tamping it firmly with the tip of her abdomen before shoveling on more loose dirt. She has gone to a great deal of trouble to catch this beef and bring it here, and she is taking care that it doesn't spoil from careless packing before her egg hatches. When the pit is full she is still not satisfied. Pulling and tugging at small sticks and bits of coal, some of them several times her size, she rearranges the landmarks until all trace of her work has disappeared.

᪥

A pile of fresh dirt the size of a tablespoon marks the place where still another wasp has been digging. She is a new one in the neighborhood—a large, thick-bodied wasp with orange body and blue wings. A wide blue and black band around the last half of her abdomen, and black markings on her shoulders and face give her a gay appearance.

Working industriously she soon had a shaft a half inch in diameter and between five and six inches deep slanting steeply downwards. When that was done, she went away to hunt.

Later she came flying back with a large green grasshopper clasped tightly underneath her body. Dropping him on the dirt pile she went down to make a few last-minute arrangements before carrying him inside. After taking care of the business in her cellar, she carelessly filled the shaft but made no effort to scatter the fresh dirt that was left.

During the night it rained and all the next day was wet, so she did not work. However, the following morning the sun came out hot, and late in the forenoon the orange wasp came back and cleared out the shaft. This was a surprising performance, for the other wasps seem to forget their diggings as soon as they've brought home a spider or caterpillar and buried it with an egg. Almost at once she replugged the burrow and went away for the day, perhaps because it was coming up to rain.

The following day she reopened the burrow again and brought in two more grasshoppers before closing the place for good. The hoppers were each as large or larger than the old wasp, so her young ones must have terrific appetites. Against one little bank in the yard she built three more nurseries, stocked each with three hoppers, and then no more was seen of her or of any wasp like her.

Weed Patch

Not all of the dooryard's business goes on around the bushes, the trees, or even on the bare ground around the doorsteps. Along one side of the sunny slope at the edge of the lot, the weeds and grass have been left to grow as they please. This wild tangle does not particularly please the neighbors who admire close-cropped lawns, but it is a richly stocked small-game preserve.

On hot mornings there is a constant going and coming at all levels. The bumblebees go from blossom to blossom overhead gathering pollen until they have great yellow masses in the baskets on their hind legs. When one flies off to the nest in the ground under the pile of dead grass cuttings, another comes to take her place. Wasps hover endlessly in the hot green light just under the weed tops, inspecting the stems and undersides of leaves and blossoms. The spider hunters, especially, do a big business here.

These are not fighting spiders, and if the wasp misses on her first pass at him, her victim usually drops to the ground and plays possum—so all she has to do is drop down after him, sting him, and carry him off.

But now and again a wasp runs up against a spider made of sterner stuff.

A mud dauber, discovering a garden spider in a nearby weed, struck like a hawk; but the spider saw her in

57

time and dropped out of sight below this jungle roof. The wasp zoomed down through the weed tops to search the ground below, not realizing that the spider had landed on a leaf a foot above the ground. While her enemy ran excitedly around below her, the spider peered cautiously over the edge of her perch. Then, when the wasp, casting frantically about in wider and wider circles, went out of sight for a moment, she made a great leap to another leaf, and from there to the ground. A spider can move fast when it has to, and this one hustled for the shadows under the privet hedge at top speed without a backward glance.

A wasp may work in the hot sun for an hour at a time, examining hundreds of possible hiding places before she finds a spider, so she does dislike to lose one. This particular mud dauber seemed to feel sure her intended victim was somewhere close by, and in her search time after time she covered every inch of the ground for several feet around. She looked under every leaf and under each bit of dead grass and broken weed stem, then searched all those places again. Convinced at last that there must be another answer, she took to the air once more.

❧§❧

Down by the grass roots a small spider has caught a middle-sized green caterpillar. The spider has a high forehead, is about the size of the end of my little finger, and sports a coat of dark yellow-orange fur, so he looks much like a small, misshapen lion. When I come upon the pair, the butchery has already been done, and the spider is ready to eat. But everywhere about are the small black ants that make our own picnics miserable, and the spider apparently knows all about them, for he immediately begins to drag his prize up into the branches of some nearby grass. After considerable struggle he manages to get the caterpillar firmly placed across the fork of a limb, a good two inches above the ground and the inquisitive ants. Then, after washing his face and front feet which seem to have gotten soiled during his work, he sets about sucking the juice from his victim.

But even though he has escaped the attention of the ants, the spider is not allowed to eat in peace, for a small gray and black fly soon comes to join him. At first the fly investigates the end of the caterpillar farthest from the place where the spider is working. Then he licks the oozings from the parts of the caterpillar that were bruised during the struggle on the ground. But before long the hot sun has dried these spots, and the fly has no way to break through the caterpillar's skin to get at the juice inside. So he goes up to face the spider as if to ask for another straw.

But when he comes too close, the spider simply reaches out one of his long forelegs and taps the fly gently on the head. The fly goes away but is soon back, watching hungrily. The caterpillar is shrinking visibly under the fly's feet, but each time the fly tries to partake of the feast, he gets tapped on the back for his pains. So he waits as patiently as he can until the spider finishes, dropping the remains of his meal to the ground. Now at last the fly is free to harvest any last drops of caterpillar juice—but it's a mighty slender meal and he soon goes off to harass someone else.

After eating, the spider washes carefully, like a cat, then climbs deliberately down from his perch and walks onto a small leaf lying on the ground. Reaching an edge of the leaf, he grasps it with his feet and swings, head first, down and under, like an acrobat coming off a net. Underneath he has several sheets of tough webbing, making a long envelope which, slung hammock-fashion under the curl of the leaf, makes a watertight roof over his quarters.

Crawling in through the narrow slit at one end, he sleeps comfortably with two or three layers of the fine silk under him to keep off cold and damp from the ground below, and the silk covers above to ward off draft. It is a pleasant thing to think of him safe there on nights when the rain drums on the roof.

Outside, as he goes at his hunting, there is always the chance that wasps or other enemies may pick him off, but once in his hammock he is pretty safe from everything—except from the danger of being crushed by some heavy-footed person walking by.

ᢤᢥ

This small wildlife business is much like watching a six-ringed circus—before you can finish watching one thing, at the other end of the tent another attraction even more interesting catches your eye. So now, while the tiger beetles race about looking for more victims, a movement down in the grass close by demands attention. A thin, black, inch-long wasp with a thread waist and dusty red band about her abdomen is plodding by, straddling a caterpillar longer than herself. She threads her way between the stalks of grass, walks under some of the dead leaves and over others. It is rough going, but in a quarter of an hour she has made fifty feet, finally reaching the edge of a honeysuckle tangle by the grapevine. A wasp dragging a spider may drop her load every few feet and hurry on ahead to take a look at the place she has already prepared, making sure all is in order before she hurries back to pick up her groceries again. But this caterpillar hunter is more single-minded, and the only time she lets loose of her burden is when the caterpillar gets tangled in a bunch of grass and she must take a new grip in order to jerk him free.

She had evidently come some distance when I first met

her, for the caterpillar already showed considerable wear and was pretty well plastered with dirt.

A palm-sized clearing at the edge of the honeysuckle was her goal, and she missed it by a little, having to back-track six inches or so. She cast about to the right for half that distance before she found her diggings—not bad navigation in such thick timber.

Laying the caterpillar down, the wasp made a few last minute changes in the tunnel construction and then helped him in, finally leaving him one of her eggs for company. After that she filled the shaft and carefully camouflaged it.

It was a beautiful job, but I couldn't help thinking that she would have done much better to have first caught her caterpillar and then looked for the nearest satisfactory place to dig the nest he was to supply food for. It would have saved her a great many steps. And as far as I could see, the place where she had so forehandedly dug the tunnel was no better than a dozen others she passed on the way. However, she may have had a perfectly good reason that I knew nothing about.

Directly or indirectly, the lives of all living things depend on the soil. The plants draw up raw materials that have dissolved in water around their roots and eventually reach the leaves. The plant eaters, insect as well as animal, cannot obtain food directly from the soil, but get it second-hand by feeding on plants. Others, the ones that cannot draw energy from either the soil or from the plants, are forced to get theirs thirdhand by eating the flesh of the vegetarians, or each other. But the soil is only a thin layer on the surface of sterile Earth, and it must be constantly replenished or everyone will starve. So it is the law that everything that dies must be returned to the soil as quickly as possible, to be broken down for reuse by the plants. And disabled creatures, too, must be disposed of when their usefulness is past. So while the hunters go about their bloody work of keeping the numbers of each other in check, another crew is busy cleaning up after them.

The small black ants are everywhere, running this way and that in apparently aimless fashion. One, scouting by himself, comes across the trail of a small beetle crippled in some battle earlier in the day. One of his wing covers is torn off, and in the hard shell of his thorax is a tiny triangular puncture that might have been made by a bird's beak. How the word spreads it is impossible to tell, but soon there are two ants, then a few others—until a dozen or more are running excitedly around the beetle like wolves around a wounded buffalo. Now and then the beetle turns at bay, threatening the ants in front of him or trying to brush away the ones who have swarmed onto his back and are tearing at his wound.

If the hurt is bad enough the ants will continue to gather in numbers until at last they bring him down. Then they will butcher him on the spot, carrying his flesh away until at last nothing is left but his empty shell.

Working here, there, and everywhere in the grass, these tiny ants clear away a wide variety of dead and disabled insects, burying the remains in their burrows underground. These are the same ants that annoy us by coming to our picnics, swarming over our food and trying to make off with it. But they do not deliberately try to make pests of themselves; they are only doing the housekeeping job they were made for. Nobody ever told them picnics were not included in the list of things that are to be cleaned up and buried.

·ᴈᵹᵉᴂ·

The sexton beetles take care of the carcasses of small birds, snakes, and other creatures too large for the ants to deal with. A pair of these handsome yellow and black beetles, coming across a dead mouse in the weeds, examine him closely and then set to work to bury him. To do a job like that you or I would dig a hole near by, put the mouse in it, and then cover the hole with dirt. But the beetle has a system that suits him better. He and his mate simply crawl under their find and start loosening the dirt, shoving it out to the sides as they work. There is no toting and hauling or running about as there is around the workings of the wasps or ants.

The only signs of activity here are occasional small shiftings and heavings as the mouse slowly sinks and the ridge of loose earth rises around his body. After a time the mouse sinks lower than the surface of the ground and the ridge begins to crumble and fall on top of him. It is a self-filling hole these beetles dig, and when they have finished there will be nothing but a small area of loosened earth to mark the spot where the mouse disappeared.

And having neatly disposed of a carcass that would otherwise have soon become offensive, they settle down to collect their pay. They will lay their eggs right there, and when the young beetles hatch the whole family will live comfortably for many weeks in the same hole with this handy food supply.

Occasional Visitors

Beside the regular population, there are others who live close by and only come to the dooryard every now and then for the hunting. They go about their affairs so quietly people seldom realize they are about.

During the hot, dry weather the old blacksnake often comes into the yard for water. And while he is in the neighborhood he makes use of his time by looking about for eggs or small birds. There are a good many trees and bushes here, and searching each one takes time, so he doesn't harm the bird population to speak of. He also goes under the house and takes care of the mouse situation, in case a family has happened to move in since his last visit. All in all, he is as little trouble as the average guest.

As he spends a hot afternoon stretched out on a branch of the privet outside the window, the catbird complains and fusses at him a little. And the wrens discuss him in loud voices for a few minutes if they come across him suddenly. But they soon lose interest and drift away.

As a general thing, the creatures a snake meets show no particular pleasure in making his acquaintance, and he governs himself accordingly. But now and again he meets an individualist who doesn't follow the rules. A pet chicken has owned the yard, for all practical purposes, all spring.

He was one of those Easter gifts misguided folk so often give to children at this particular time of year. But instead of quietly fading away as most of them do, this chicken developed into an aggressive character, prospering on his own with no social contacts except people. In almost no time he had grown feathers and refused to be penned up. The yard was inches deep in rotting leaves and trash which harbored an amazing population of grubs, beetles, and other such game. The chicken spent his days turning over the damp leaf piles and chasing the startled bugs that live there with loud cries of delight. And the exercise and the diet seemed to agree with him, so much so that by the middle of summer he was a truly formidable chicken, lord of all he surveyed. Even the cats and dogs stepped aside for this arrogant bird.

One hot noontime the blacksnake came prospecting quietly around the house, looking for a shady spot. Being inquisitive, as snakes often are, he came up the steps to peer through the screen door that opens onto the porch. Then his attention was attracted by sounds of the chicken approaching, coming around the house from the other direction. In the dry top leaves the chicken stepped like Jack-in-the-Beanstalk's giant, making a noise all out of proportion to his size. The snake held his ground, waiting to see what was coming. Discovering it was only a chicken he began to relax visibly, for past experience had shown him that in such cases a bird usually stands off at a safe distance, making loud, threatening or alarmed noises. After a decent interval, the snake would then be allowed to go away, slowly and quietly. But this chicken, having been brought up with people, was inexperienced in such matters. So far, everything he'd found crawling on the ground had been fair game—even the big four-inch-long centipedes.

So instead of hesitating at the sight of four feet of

snake draped over the steps, he gave a pleased-sounding war whoop and rushed up to harvest the huge worm he'd found! This unorthodox reaction completely upset the snake, who whipped back down the path and around the corner of the house with the chicken in full cry behind him. A snake can disappear with great suddenness if there is cover of any kind around. By the time the chicken had turned the corner in pursuit, the yard appeared deserted. Where the snake went is not known. Maybe he crawled under the house, maybe under the leaves or pine straw. There were any number of possibilities, but the chicken apparently believed he was under the half-buried tile protecting the water cutoff, and he mumbled and complained around it for a half hour. The biggest worm he'd ever seen —and it got away.

Later, another individualist, a jay this time, gave the snake a bad time. This happened in one of the two big oak trees in front of the house. Apparently the snake had been surprised by the jay as he was trying to make his way overhead from one tree to the other. Now he had balled himself up, with both ends tucked in out of harm's way, at the tip end of a branch about twenty feet from the ground. With the snake in defensive position, he had the jay at a disadvantage, which the bird seemed to realize, for he hushed his clamor and quietly examined the situation. He appeared to have no fear of the snake suddenly taking the offensive, for he moved unhurriedly from one twig to another, only inches away from the black coils. Deciding at last that there was no place he could take hold of this intruder he flew to another branch, there to work on his feathers a bit. Then he moved off down the street, stopping for a while at each tree to make a few choice remarks at the top of his lungs before going on to the next tree. So it was easy to trace his progress as the racket he made grew fainter and fainter. It disappeared altogether somewhere in the next block.

Maybe the snake was listening to the departing blue jay, and maybe he wasn't. But if he was, he probably figured, as I did, that the jay was long gone. But perhaps he had dealt with jays before, so for fifteen minutes or more he made no move to expose himself. By the time he did stir, cautiously bringing his head out to look about, the jay had already come ghosting back and was sitting motionless on the limb of a tree not far away.

The snake carefully examined the nearby branches, always ready to jerk his head back should anything move. Later, he disarranged his tight loops a little in order to raise his head a couple of inches higher for a better view. And all the time the jay watched him from his perch without making a sound or movement of any kind. Little by little the snake gained courage. He loosened up until he was able to see all around as well as above and below, and still there was no sign of the bird.

Finally, convinced there was nothing to fear, he began to stretch the front end of his body out into space, measuring the distance to the nearest branch of the adjoining tree. Each time he failed to reach it he hauled himself back, rearranging his remaining loops to get more slack. And each time, before making another try, he peered suspiciously about the surrounding branches, looking for the jay. This was truly a delicate piece of business he was engaged in. Each time he loosed another coil so as to add to his reach, the load on the remaining coils which gripped the slender branch was increased, as was the danger of a slip. But at last he had the distance measured. If he could just get his chin over the farther branch, it would be a simple matter for him to flow across the gap.

All this time the jay was a silent but interested spectator. And now, when the snake had extended himself to his very limit, the bird moved. Hopping unhurriedly down to another branch within a couple of inches of the straining coils, he examined them carefully. Then, after a sidewise glance to make sure he hadn't been noticed, he hauled himself up and hit the tip of the snake's tail just one sledge hammer blow with his powerful beak. There is no way of knowing just how tender a snake's tail is. But anyone who has seen a jay hammer a nut or acorn to open it will realize that a whack like that must have been a mighty shock to the snake's entire system. At any rate, the snake tried to jerk his tail out of reach of this dreadful attack and immediately lost his grip on the branch.

His fall to the ground was no serious matter, and a bruised tail would not permanently disable him, but he seemed far from pleased as he scuttled under the ivy and out of sight for the day. It is small wonder snakes dislike blue jays.

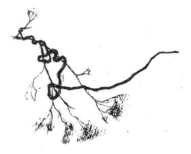

In this business of watching wildlife working at its trade, it is sometimes a little difficult to be sure who is watching whom. Every now and then the watcher finds that he himself is being watched.

The other day a small king snake and I met at the crossing of a little ditch at the bottom of the yard. He was just slithering down the far bank as I arrived. Seeing me, he followed the custom of snakes in such situations, "freezing" where he was, planning to wait until I had gone by.

With his head flat on the leaves in the bottom of the

ditch and most of himself disposed in loose kinks up the side of the far bank, he was almost invisible—as long as he remained motionless. And, for the next fifteen minutes or so, nobody moved as the snake and I waited each other out.

In the case of this encounter, it was the snake who moved first. He raised his head just a little, then waited to see what would happen. When nothing did, he cautiously raised it a little higher, watching me with a bright, inquisitive look as I sat on the bank above him. He seemed to be uncertain whether I was dangerous or not, now that I had not moved for so long, but he was still suspicious. Maybe if he threatened me a little he could stir up some action and find out for sure if I was something alive. So, raising his head still higher, he made small threatening, bobbing motions in my direction—then froze again to await results. This went on for another quarter of an hour until at last he seemed satisfied that I was harmless and started hauling his coils down from the steep ditch bank to the bottom. And then, instead of going on about his interrupted hunting, he climbed directly up my side of the bank. Coming to one of my shoes, he began to examine it closely, going around the edge of the sole inch by inch, tasting and smelling it with his sensitive, flickering, forked tongue. It was plain he'd never seen a shoe before and he was puzzled. After finding out all he could about the edges of the soles, he raised himself higher and began to examine the shoe tops, paying considerable attention to the dangling shoe laces. Just in case he might take a notion go on up my pantleg next, to see about my socks, I reached out and gently rubbed the underside of his chin with a twig, then lifted him back a few inches. He reacted to the stroking of his neck as a cat does, stretching and leaning against the little stick, seeming to take no offense at being pushed away. Instead, he came back and examined my other shoe. It's not every day a serpent has a chance to examine a man's shod feet at leisure, for people are notoriously timid, although they can be dangerous when cornered. After finding out all he could about both shoes and having his chin stroked again, the king snake finally seemed to decide he could take no more time from his business and moved unhurriedly away without a backward look.

Apparently, the snake was hunting grasshoppers or lizards. I watched him as he moved quietly forward, taking cover behind a pine cone or a small clump of grass. When he was in position, he would raise his neck straight up so that his head was high enough to peer over his cover and look about for game. When he was satisfied there was nothing worth while in sight, he'd flow up and over the blind and move quietly to the next lookout.

At last he disappeared in a patch of broom grass, and I went on about my own affairs.

ঙৢৢ৲

Toads destroy insects by uncounted thousands but seem to have few enemies themselves after they are full grown. Their skins secrete a bad-tasting fluid that discourages the attention of dogs, cats, and other predators. However, there always is some specialist in nature to see that no species overruns the land. In the case of toads, it is the hog-nosed snake which moves in to thin them out when the toad population becomes too heavy.

Locally, the hog-nosed snake is known as a puff adder or spreading adder, and he is supposed to be deadly poisonous. As a matter of fact, he is a harmless fellow who specializes in toad hunting.

He gets his name from the fact that he is a terrific bluffer who puts on an astonishing show when he is disturbed. He swells up, hisses, and strikes viciously at his disturber, apparently hoping to frighten the intruder off.

Then if that fails, he spreads and flattens the back of his neck in cobra fashion, holding his head high and continuing his hissing. Some people are convinced that with his hissing he sprays fine droplets of venom that will blind you if it gets in your eyes, so when he puts on his act they either kill him or go quickly away and leave him alone.

But if a person neither kills him nor goes away after the puff adder's first display, the snake still has another trick with which to fool him. He suddenly plays dead! He goes limp, opens his mouth wide to expose its fishy-white lining, and rolls over on his back. He couldn't possibly look deader. And usually he has made sure that some dirt, bits of grass, or other trash have gotten into his mouth to add to the illusion. Pick him up if you like—he still remains a snake which has just met a most dreadful end. However, he has a one-track mind: if, while he is playing dead, you happen to turn him over to examine his back, he immediately startles you by thrashing about—to turn belly-up again. He knows how a dead snake should look!

For a while a puff adder lived at the bottom of my yard, fattening himself on the toads that inhabited the old chicken yard, which was all right with me. There were more toads there than were really needed in that spot, and if they didn't like to share their home with the snake, there was no reason why they couldn't move on. As a general thing I do not interfere in such wildlife affairs, but after a while the snake moved up to take a look at the pair of toads that lived by the house.

This time something had to be done, for I couldn't spare these two. And it was time this greedy fellow went on to the neighbors to do some toad thinning for them, so I carried him some distance away, pointed him in the direction he should go, and gave him a smart rap on the tail to encourage his departure.

ᎦᏜᏜᏜ

Considering the hundreds of wasps that will normally hatch during the summer from the two wasp nests over the doorway, to say nothing of the crop from the half-dozen other nests under the eaves, for a while it looked as though the dooryard was going to have more wasps than were needed. But soon after the first hatch of small caterpillars had been thinned a little, the crested flycatcher came to hang on the screen door and look the situation over.

The brown wasp's nest had a dozen or more capped cells, marking grubs already pupating as well as other fat ones nearly full size. Carefully snipping off the stem, the bird carried the nest to the holly tree where he held it firmly with one foot while he picked out the grubs one by one.

Later, he looked at the brown and yellow wasp family, but evidently deciding it was too small to bother with, he left it to pick off several of the larger colonies elsewhere. Every week or so he comes around, and if he finds a colony with enough well-developed grubs to make the effort worth his while, he snips the nest and carries it off.

So there will be no need to spray or burn the wasps out this year.

Night Time

Late in the afternoon the orb weaver stirs in her daytime hiding place on a high limb of the juniper tree. Pushing aside the small greenery that has protected her from the sun and hunting wasps, she comes out into the open to look about to see what changes may have been made while she slept. Night after night, like a fisherman setting a net in a stream, she hangs her web to catch her night's supply of groceries.

Firmly attaching a lifeline to the branch where she stands, she slowly drops toward the ground twenty feet below. Two thirds of the way down, she stops her descent, to swing for a bit on the end of her invisible tether. Then, reaching behind her, she begins to spin out a kind of silk that is different from the lifeline. A wide, light ribbon, it floats on the air like a wisp of smoke. It drifts this way and that, upward, then downward, as its length increases, until at last the end attaches itself to the top of a strong weed several feet away. Using this line, the spider is able to pull herself over into a weed top to which she attaches the end of her life line. This solves the mystery of how she is able to set up the diagonal guy line that is the foundation of her web. Running back, part way up the diagonal, she attaches another line, then drops with it straight to the ground. Her anchor now is not the ground itself, but a little bundle of dead pine needles.

Scrambling halfway back up this last line, she stops to attach a new thread; then, holding it well away from the old, she continues her climb to the top of the V. Back down she goes for several feet, still holding her new line free. Finding a suitable place she stops, draws in the slack in the loop until the new line is taut, then attaches her end firmly to the diagonal. Now she has three sides of a rough triangle that will be the foundation of her web, high above the ground. She will add more braces here and there, then stretch the radii like spokes of a wheel and make a rough spiral scaffold of the life-line silk. She is a black dot against the sky, and except in certain lights, her silk is invisible so that she seems to be moving about at her work without support of any kind.

It may take her an hour or more to complete the job. When it is done she settles down in the center of her new web to wait for customers. The web is a handsome construction now, with every line drawn taut. Gusts of night wind may shake it, but at the end of the long, diagonal guy line the weed bends and gives. And the small bundle of pine needles that serves to anchor the other line is lifted by the straining silk, then falls back. These safety features, added to the natural elasticity of the silk network, keep the lines from breaking.

Just before dusk, about the time the spider is finishing her web overhead, the old toad makes his appearance. He has owned the hunting rights to the front doorstep for several years. Every evening in nice weather he comes out from under the holly tree, hops deliberately down the brick walk, up onto the four-inch-high stoop, and takes his place under the porch chair. As soon as the porch light is turned on, the big brown May beetles start to gather on the screen door and on the walls close by. The toad waits patiently for someone to pick them off and toss one down to him every now and then. No toad will touch game that is not moving, so the trick here is to toss the insect in such a way that it will bounce or roll within his reach. He really lives "high on the hog," that toad. There seems to be no limit to the number of May beetles he can eat at a sitting.

What he does the rest of the night is not clear, but early in the morning he is usually to be seen among the flower beds. And when the sun begins to get hot he goes over to the cool dampness of the ground under the holly tree to bury himself for the day. Scuffling around with his hind feet, he keeps shoving dirt out from under him so he has the appearance of slowly sinking into the ground. When his eyes are just below the surrounding surface, he reaches up a front foot and scrapes loose dirt over himself. This he does with a sweeping circular motion, so that he suddenly disappears as if he's pulled the hole in after him.

A smaller toad has been learning the trade at the back door, which seems to be a less desirable hunting territory than the front. Every now and again this one will prowl around the corner of the house and along the dog's path until he can see if the old toad is in his place under the porch chair. There seems to be no communication between them, but the small toad always goes back to his lonely place at the back door after he's watched a while.

Except for the spider and the toads, the yard seems deserted, but a search with a flashlight will turn up much activity. Fireflies climb out of the grass to flash signals to others flying about. And down on the ground their larvae, the glowworms, are on the prowl. They can be located by their tiny glowing lights in the dark damp under the grass, and a patient watcher may be on hand to watch them at their work. Armed with poison fangs they are able to bring down game many times larger than themselves, and they perform numerous executions among the earth worms, snails, and other slow movers.

Searching the rotting wood of the old oak stump, a curious type of millepede comes in sight. His back plates are notched ivory white and rich brown. Most of one antenna is gone, and he travels hesitatingly, like a blind man turning his head from side to side as he gently explores with the remaining one the ground in front of him. He is a gentle soul, a vegetarian feeding on decaying vegetation, helping return it to the soil as soon as possible. Touch him and he curls up tightly, his armored back protecting his soft belly and legs.

Another jointed, many-legged creature hunts the same area and is also often mistaken for the millepede.

This is the centipede, a fellow as bloodthirsty as the millepede is gentle. Instead of two pairs of legs to each segment, he has only one. He and all his relations are meat eaters. This one in the grass is sleek; his legs are short and his polished skin looks like leather rubbed with prussian blue. A relative of his is the hairy-looking fellow we often get a glimpse of as he dashes about in the shadows along the baseboards indoors, or find in the bathtub or washbasin. He is a hunter of flies, mosquitoes, and cockroaches.

Almost anywhere one looks, there is some small creature moving. Spider or beetle, a dozen kinds search the grass or hustle across the open places. A good many of the small snakes are night hunters also, although they are more difficult to see. The flashlight beam reflects bright green sparkles from mysterious insect eyes in almost any dark crevice or corner.

Mysterious Holes
in the Ground

As a general thing nobody pays much attention to small holes in the ground. Yet there are hundreds of them of almost every imaginable size in the dooryard. Some are the lairs of hunters lying in ambush and others are the hiding places of weak or timid folk. Some are permanent homesteads; others are used once or twice, then abandoned.

The neatly drilled round holes of the tiger beetles' larvae can be found in the sun-baked earth of paths and weed patches. The largest of these are less than half the size of a pencil and they drop straight downward, like tiny man-made wells.

These holes have no parapets or mounds of dirt around them, and their small dooryards seem to be neatly swept for an inch or two in all directions. The passer-by sees nothing more than the mysterious, dark entrance, apparently deserted. But push a straw gently down to the bottom of the hole, and the owner will probably grasp it with his pinchers and let you haul him close enough to the surface to recognize him. This hole in the ground with its neatly kept edges will be the young one's home and hunting lodge until he becomes a beetle.

Other mysterious holes, each surrounded by a small turret-like parapet, can be found in the flower beds, in the grass, or even in patches of pine straw. They may seem deserted, but a flashlight beam directed down a shaft of one of them will be reflected in a brilliant sparkle of green from spider eyes deep in the dark tunnel. For these are the homes of the wolf spiders, cousins of the tarantulas and trap-door spiders. A large wolf spider lives beside the walk, only a few feet from the porch steps.

Except for the parapet, carefully made of odd bits of grass, pine needles, sticks or bits of dirt fastened in place with silk, there is nothing particularly fancy about her home. A shaft the size of the spider's body drops straight down into the ground for six inches or thereabouts. The walls are cemented with saliva or silk to prevent cave-ins as the spider runs up and downstairs.

During the day she spends long hours leaning over the edge of her parapet, soaking up the sun and watching the country roundabout. If some uninformed insect happens to blunder within reach while she is thus occupied she will make short work of him, but most of her hunting is done at night. Then, with a flashlight one can surprise her hustling about the neighborhood, tracking down beetles and other insects.

When she has run down a victim and butchered him, she usually totes the carcass home, down to the very bottom of her burrow where she can eat in peace. Occasionally, in the morning one finds shiny bits of beetle shell scattered around her dooryard. This may happen when she has had to partly dismantle a visitor too large to go through her doorway and down her hall in one piece. As a general thing she never throws anything out. After she has sucked some juicy creatures dry, she pushes the remaining shells together as neatly as possible, like a cook discarding used eggshells, and stuffs them into a corner or leaves them underfoot. She is truly a dreadful housekeeper. An old wolf spider burrow will sometimes contain a whole tablespoonful of beetle shells, empty wasp carcasses, and such refuse lying on the floor. But in spite of her bloodthirsty nature and sorry housekeeping habits, the wolf spider is an entertaining neighbor.

For a while the one who lived by our doorstep carried a small, dirty-white, buckshot-sized pouch with her wherever she went—upstairs and down, and even on her hunting trips. It contained her year's eggs, and until her young ones hatched she was a most attentive mother. Then one morning we notice she seems to have changed color. Her velvety, brownish-black has changed to a scuffy, nondescript gray, as though she has contracted some kind of skin disease. But a closer look shows that something quite different has happened. She no longer carries her purse of eggs; instead a hundred or more unbelievably small spiders now cling to her back.

As far as it is possible to tell, she makes no attempt to feed her offspring—she pays little attention to them in fact. She suns herself as usual and at the same time suns the young ones. Whe she goes hunting at night, the whole crowd goes along on her back. But if some of the baby spiders fall off or wander away, as they occasionally do, it would seem to the observer that she doesn't even notice. This is probably just as well, for if she tried to count and keep track of such a brood she would soon be in a mighty nervous state. Apparently the protection of the egg sac was her big concern. Now she only waits patiently for the day the young ones will leave so that she can have her house to herself once more and no longer has to feel the patter of hundreds of little feet scampering across her back.

Like many people who leave the dishes unwashed, floors unswept, and their beds unmade, but keep the yard raked and the brass doorknob polished, the wolf spider spends much of her time improving the outside of her property. When she enlarges her hallway, as she must now and then do to take care of a gain in weight, she doesn't throw the dirt where it will mess up her yard. Instead, she brings it to the surface in neat little pellets and scatters them some distance off. And she is everlastingly repairing and adding to her watchtower. Sometimes, after a long spell of wet weather, the material she is using apparently gets musty and begins to displease her. When this occurs, she cuts the silk that anchors it to the ground and hauls the whole construction away, to discard it like an empty barrel.

Rain doesn't bother this wolf spider for often she will sit just inside her doorway during a heavy shower. At other times she will try experiments with doors themselves. One day her doorway was crisscrossed with a fine, lacy web net. What purpose the net served is anybody's guess. At other times, for reasons of her own, she will tear down her watchtower, using the material to make a cover to seal the doorway. After she has finished this operation she may not appear for a couple of weeks.

⋖⧉⋗

Early in the summer another kind of mysterious hole often may be found in the hard-packed ground of the dooryard, usually near the roots of a tree. It is half an inch in diameter and, from what one is able to see, the walls of the shaft look as though they have been smoothly plastered with mud. But in spite of the neat finish, this hole will not be used again. It marks the end of the thirteen- or seventeen-year underground journey of a cicada grub.

Hatched from eggs laid in the bark of a twig high overhead, the young cicada immediately drops to the ground and burrows deep into the earth. He makes his way through the ground in much the same way the mole does, opening a passage ahead of him with his powerful front feet and shoving the dirt behind him. For years he cruises about far below the earth's surface, sucking the sap from the tree roots he finds about him. Then, after a certain number of years, without consulting either a calendar or clock, he suddenly decides it is time to change his ways. Digging his way to the surface, he may or may not be surprised to discover that after about seventeen years underground, he has picked the one suitable month of the year for his appearance out in the world.

He wastes no time peering about to admire the view, for he has much to do. He walks to the nearest tree or bush and crawls up a little way; then he takes a death grip on the bark and settles down to make the change from brownish humpbacked grub to a brilliant-winged cicada.

The process takes some time. For a while nothing seems to be happening. Then the grub's shell begins to split over the hump of his shoulders and slowly down his back. A struggle starts as the insect inside bulges and squirms, trying to work itself through the narrow slit in the armor in which it is encased. Little by little the head of the insect comes free; one by one its legs are pulled out of the old coverings, like a man removing his boots. Now an insect's skeleton is on the outside, so until the air hardens his new shell, this moulting cicada's body is soft and pliable. Otherwise, he would never be able to get out of his old coat.

After much struggle he is finally free and crawls at last into the sunlight to rest and finish his development. Little by little, his shell hardens and takes on color. His wings expand and dry as his body fluids are forced, under pressure, through his veins—and, in a surprisingly short time, he has become a brilliant creature—bearing little resemblance to the muddy brown shell that will remain hooked to the bark of bush or tree where this transformation took place.

⊷§⊱

Now that the sun is out again after three days of cold, rainy weather, the mole comes to hunt in the dooryard. Almost everybody knows of the mole because of the ridges he makes in the lawn and flower beds, but not many realize that he is a hunter. We say of many creatures that they live in the ground, meaning that they sleep, raise their families, and perhaps store food there. But the mole is one who truly inhabits the ground almost as completely as the shark inhabits the sea. His living quarters are a series of well-constructed galleries a foot or two below ground. When he is hungry he moves upstairs, but instead of going outside he cruises about just below the earth's surface, among the roots of plants, searching for the worms and insects which feed there also.

Now, with the sun shining, a small ridge appears around the corner of the porch, moving jerkily this way and that through the sandy soil. The mole travels with a sort of swimming motion, forcing one or another of his big shovel-shaped front feet ahead of his snout to shove the dirt aside and in back of him. By turning his body and humping his back, he compresses the dirt on each side and at the same time raises a roof overhead to make a passage for his body. The tip of the ridge seems to move by itself, this way

and that, with many starts and stops, around the roots of
the marigold, along the line of the pansy bed, then by zig-
zag ways from one small grass tussock to another. Each
short stop probably marks the violent end of another earth-
worm, beetle, or other insect the mole has surprised in the
damp darkness. He sets no speed records as he paddles
through the loose soil, but the game he hunts is neither fast
nor wary, so he does all right.

After a time the slowly moving ridge disappears under
a pile of sand and leaves beside the compost pit. For a
while nothing happens; then the exposed end of a half-
buried piece of dead wood begins a curious series of small
jerkings and heavings. Another spell of quiet, and then
small subterranean disturbances crack the rain-packed
crust of the dirt pile on the farther side of the yard, a
couple of feet away.

By watching for these cracks and shiftings, it is possible to follow the mole's progress as he goes about his business. From side to side and from one level to another, he
searches for the rich harvest of insects drawn by the rotting
leaves or driven underground by the cold rain.

After half an hour or more he seems to have exhausted the possibilities of the dirt pile, and again the tip of
the little ridge moves out into the open. This time it investigates a row of half-buried bricks. The ridge disappears
under one edge of a brick, which heaves and shifts almost
imperceptibly for a few moments; then the ridge appears at
the far side again and moves on.

At the first footfall in the neighborhood the mole
turns and digs downwards to the safety of the deeper galleries, and the little ridge appears to stop its searching.

The mole's hunting galleries are used only once, as a
general thing. But mice, beetles, and many other creatures
may make use of them, and, because they often eat the

roots of plants the mole was freeing of pests, give him a bad name with gardeners.

Every now and again some curious, window-like holes the size of a nickel appear in the steep sides of a pile of sandy earth in the weed patch. They are most mysterious, for it is plain that they open into a small tunnel in the sand, but there is no sign on the outside to show how they were made. It takes considerable patient investigating to learn that they are the work of the whip-tailed lizard.

This lizard often comes quietly across the hot sand of the dooryard to hunt under the little patches of pine straw, or under the fat plantain leaves, or in the variegated litter around the bushes. Earth worms, caterpillars, grubs, and even small beetles—all look good to him. Apparently he has no teeth, so when he catches a creature too large to swallow at a gulp, he has a problem on his hands. He sets up a great commotion in the leaves as he pecks and beats some soft-bodied victim, fraying him out to bite-sized scraps.

Ordinarily the whip-tailed lizard doesn't scurry about as nervously as do the smaller anole and fence lizard. But when he does feel like hurrying, he raises upright and runs on his hind legs, balanced by his long tail. Instead of going under the leaf mold to sleep as the other lizards do, he often tunnels into the sand. After he has brought his galleries almost to the earth's surface in several places, he goes back and carefully closes his original entrance.

The window-like openings he sometimes makes at the end of a hallway may be for the purpose of ventilation. On very hot days or in cold, rainy weather, he bulldozes sand from the tunnel floor and plugs them up. In time of danger it takes him only a fraction of a second to open a new doorway, so that he seems to explode out of the solid ground in a small shower of sand. He goes away at top speed while his enemy is still searching for him elsewhere.

Autumn—The Quiet Season

Some mornings hundreds of fine gossamer streamers float out from every tree and bush in the yard; and other hundreds sail aimlessly overhead. Everywhere the sparkle of sunlight reflects from the almost-invisible threads mystifies the neighbors.

But there is no mystery. Young spiders by the thousands are going out into the world to seek their fortunes. Each one is so small as to be nearly invisible, but the home grounds are overcrowded, and under such conditions relatives will eat one another and never give the matter a second thought. So to avoid this, the spiders search for small elevations—the top of a grass blade, the handle of the shovel stuck in the soil of a flower bed—any place where the sun, warming the earth, has set up a gently rising air current will do. When the spiders have found such a spot, they turn and spin out the fine silk line that floats so gracefully this way and that. Foot by foot, a line is let out until at last its buoyancy is great enough to lift the small spider into the air. Dangling from the homemade parachute, he may rise as high as a thousand feet and travel a hundred miles. Or his line may catch on a nearby grass blade and have to be abandoned.

With thousands of spiders on the move, it is not surprising that gossamer seems almost to be a part of the air itself.

While the young spiders are floating off to search for homes, the squirrels begin their fall harvest of acorns and pine cones. The cones cannot be stored, so they are eaten on the spot. While they are still green the squirrels cut them loose one at a time and carry them to some convenient perch for shucking. Balancing the heavy cone across a branch, the squirrel chisels off the tough scales one at a time, starting at the bottom, like a man eating an artichoke. As each scale is torn away the winged seed underneath is exposed and greedily eaten. The squirrels also spend much of their time in the oak trees, feeding on the small acorns which contain the rich, deep-yellow meat or burying them under the matted pine straw.

Now that autumn is on the way, every day a strange squirrel makes several trips past the dooryard. He lives down the hill across the street, but somehow he has discovered a pecan tree in the opposite direction, another half block away. So he comes by five or six times a day, passing my yard without a second glance. Later, he comes back with his loot, usually two pecans on the same stem. The stem gripped in his jaws, and a green pecan beside either cheek, he has a most curious appearance. With such a load he finds it unhandy to travel through the branches, so he makes the whole trip—nearly a block and a half—on foot.

At this season even the jays have interrupted their noisy affairs long enough to bury a good share of the acorn crop. Carrying two acorns in his beak at one time a jay drops onto the grass outside the window. He puts both acorns on the ground while he looks about; then, satisfied that no one is watching, he makes a hole in the ground with two or three vigorous blows of his beak, selects one of the acorns, and pokes it firmly to the bottom of the hole. After he has covered it up with dirt, he walks about, selecting and discarding leaves and small sticks until he finds one that exactly suits him. This he lays over his buried acorn, then stands back to consider it. Sometimes he moves it two or three times, a fraction of an inch this way or that, before he is satisfied with his work. Then he carries the remaining acorn off and repeats the same performance elsewhere.

With the beginning of fall there is a change in the sleeping arrangements around the dooryard. During the summer almost everyone camps out in any spot that happens to take his fancy, as some will do for the winter. But the first chilly nights start a good many looking for winter quarters.

There are no hollow trees in the yard, so all summer the young squirrels have lived here and there in hastily built, ramshackle leaf nests that were continually falling apart or blowing away. The squirrels are better-than-average weather prophets. A commotion in the trees overhead, accompanied by the fall of fresh-cut, leafy twigs, where the squirrels are busy re-thatching, warns of rain—a signal to bring the chairs in out of the yard. Running back and forth in the high branches, the squirrels cut off twigs having a spray of three or four leaves which they hustle to jam into a convenient tree crotch. When a considerable pile is in place, a squirrel will push into the leaf mass headfirst, then stir around inside until he has made a cavity to suit him. Of course, a good bit of his material is dislodged in the process, but that seems not to matter—there are plenty of leaves for the gathering. Once the framework is built it is time to thatch the nest to make it windproof. Squirrels put their roofs on the inside of their houses, not outside as you or I would do. Bringing a twig, leafy end foremost, they push it through the doorway; then they themselves seem to roll and squirm inside, so that the leaves mat and interlock to make a tight weatherproof roll, with a hollow in the middle for the squirrels to sleep in.

But with the coming of winter they build a more substantial dwelling. Probably they have learned a lot from the summer's practice, but the new nests must be larger—strong enough to stand the winter storms without coming apart.

The nest of an old female squirrel abandoned after raising a litter of young ones stands vacant for a while. Then one afternoon the wrens look in and immediately set up an outraged clamor. While the small squirrels lived there, these nosey birds were in the habit of stopping to peer in at them whenever they happened to be passing (and they seemed to make it a point to pass by at least once a day). Apparently they were just being neighborly, for they never raised any outcry at the sight of small squirrels. So it

is plain now that a tramp must have moved into the abandoned squirrel nest. A little poking with a fish pole, while the wrens scream and jitter approvingly a short distance away, brings the sound of grumbling and growling from inside. After a bit more insistence from the fish pole, a possum pokes his head out to see what is wanted. The grapes are ripe in the nearby vines, and he probably sees no need of commuting to the honeysuckle tangle every day while there is a vacant apartment handy.

A scattering of bright wood chips under the hurricane-damaged chinaberry tree in back of the studio marks the workings of the downy woodpecker. This is the third year she has wintered in this old tree, but each summer the branch she had chosen, weakened by her drilling, has broken off, so she must build a new place each fall. She makes the entrance to her home, about the size of a silver dollar, on the underside of a sloping branch and hollows out a pocket six or eight inches deep below it. She pecks and taps inside for a while, then backs up her hallway, making rapid scratching movements with her feet to rake the chips out of her way, finally kicking them out of the door. It usually takes her two or three days to finish the place to her satisfaction. But at last she is ready for the winter. No matter how rainy or cold the weather may be, she is out early in the morning and stays away at her work all day. About dusk she comes back and checks the bark of a few trees while looking about before settling down for the night. Rain or snow makes no difference to her. Fluffing her feathers a little, she fills the bottom of her small home. The porous wood of the half-rotted branch acts as insulation, and neither drafts nor hunters can reach her.

If I tap the bark outside when she is sleeping and shine a flashlight into her doorway, the woodpecker comes to the door and peers out, looking as furious as any householder disturbed in the night. If nothing more is said or done, she blinks a couple of times, then drops down to her bed to her interrupted sleep.

Fresh ravelings showing the frayed portion of an old

piece of rope hanging from the pine tree is a sign the flying squirrel has returned to his winter quarters in the bird house. Every fall he comes from down in the swamp where he spends the summer, checking into the house the tufted titmice used during the summer months. Every fall he cuts bits off the high-swinging rope, raveling it out and stuffing it into the bird house. In the middle of this fluffy mass he makes a pocket in which he sleeps out the winter days, the covers pulled over his head to keep out the light and cold drafts.

After the grapes were gone, the possum went back to the vacant lot across the street and the squirrels' nest was vacant once more—until a flicker discovered it. It isn't as satisfactory a sleeping place as a hole in a tree, but when there is a shortage of suitable places a bird has to do the best he can. So on cold nights, in the blue dusk, he comes in, rustling around inside awhile to get comfortable before settling down for the night.

One of the wrens discovers a vireo's nest, still attached to a forked branch which I had once fastened to the wall of the house by the door. On cold nights she comes quickly

but secretively around the house and onto the porch and is in the nest before anyone notices her. Our ordinary comings and goings do not seem to disturb her, but she would certainly startle anyone who happened to notice the nest in the shadows of the porch and reached out to examine it more closely.

It would seem to be a simple matter to find the sleeping places of the perching birds by searching the overhead branches of trees by flashlight. But a bird's light-colored undersides make him difficult to see from the ground below. With practice, however, the sleeping birds become visible. A dove sleeps every night in the angled mass of an evergreen bush in one corner of the yard. The leaves overhead keep off the rain, and the movement of the slender twigs underneath warn her of any close enemy. She is used to being spied on and blinks timidly in the beam of the flashlight, but she seldom does more than shift her feet a little.

When there is threat of cold rain or snow in the air, the titmice and some other small birds move into a place just over the studio door. A pine branch there has somehow accumulated a heavy mass of dead pine needles. A light flashed upward in the night may show as many as half a dozen white, feathery undersides and tail feathers sticking out of shadowy places. Neither rain nor snow can touch the birds that sleep here. Sparrows and other small birds have discovered that behind the mass of climbing ivy the bricks of the fireplace stay warm.

>>>>

Gradually the dooryard settles down to winter routines. The wasps are dead by the thousands, except for the young queens sleeping in the dark spaces between the house walls while they wait for spring and the beginning of their lonely jobs.

The mocker warms himself atop the chimney on afternoons when the fire in the fireplace inside burns low or sings a little from the ridge of the roof while he keeps an eye on the neighborhood. Now and again he chases the thrush around the house just so there will be no mistake about who owns the place. When he is bored by these small activities, he may sit just outside the window, peering inside to watch whatever work happens to be in progress. Or he may raise a fearful clatter by walking on the tin roof of the studio, listening to his favorite radio programs through the unplugged nail holes.

The old wolf spider stays in business later than most of her kind, but when the ground begins to get really cold she gathers bits of leaves and broken pine needles and glues them together into a tight mat which she uses to close her door against the cold and rain. If passers-by, tramping overhead, accidentally tear her storm door apart, she comes up later, patiently gathers up the pieces, and sticks them together.

The busy season is over, but no matter how closely the doings of the dooryard wildlife were watched, there are dozens of small mysteries still unsolved. The hummingbird came regularly to the flowers by the porch from somewhere down by the grapevine, and later he and his mate brought their young ones, but the location of the nest remains a mystery.

A big black wasp with creamy-white markings scrapes material off the dried clay in the driveway, wetting it with saliva until she has a ball of clay to carry off to a secret spot. A half hour's detective work traced her to a stump of bamboo about a foot and a half in height. She was just finishing putting a plug in the hollow top, trowelling it smooth with her mandibles. When she needed more clay she had always flown to the driveway, but now and again she would stop work to fly off in the opposite direction. Coming back she seems to be carrying a mouthful of some liquid she applies, a drop at a time, to the surface of the plug before continuing her trowelling. Perhaps it is water, but if so, it appears to have some slightly gummy substance mixed with it. At any rate, when the wasp has finished, the end of the plug shows a smooth, completely waterproof surface. She is a placid type, working with no fuss and none of the nervous buzzing of the mud daubers.

Later, when the bamboo section was opened, it revealed three nursery chambers, one above the other. The bottom one, the first one filled, held twenty-four small, pale-pink and yellow-green caterpillars and an egg. Above them was a thin clay disk or plug, a quarter-inch empty space, and another disk serving as the floor of the second nursery chamber. This second one held twenty-six small caterpillars of the same kind and an egg. The top section was separated by an empty space from both the chamber below and the plug to the outside. It held only fifteen of the caterpillars, but it also contained a fat grub that appeared to have come from the nest of a paper wasp. Another mystery. Does the black wasp make a practice of robbing other wasps to feed her young ones, or had she found this grub by accident? And where does she nest when there is no bamboo handy? Maybe next summer will tell.

Index

VR